The Adult
Faith Formation
Library

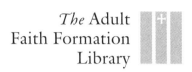

EXPLORING *the* OLD TESTAMENT

Creation, Covenant, Prophecy, Kingship

ANDREW R. DAVIS

TWENTY-THIRD
PUBLICATIONS
twentythirdpublications.com

For
HONEY AND POPPY

TWENTY-THIRD PUBLICATIONS

One Montauk Avenue, Suite 200, New London, CT 06320
(860) 437-3012 » (800) 321-0411 » www.twentythirdpublications.com

Cover photo: Shutterstock.com

ISBN: 978-1-62785-384-2
Library of Congress Catalog Card Number: 2018943229
Printed in the U.S.A.

A division of Bayard, Inc.

The Adult Faith Formation Library

Formation in our faith tradition is an ongoing endeavor; allowing this learning to inform our minds, to touch our hearts, and to find expression in the way we live is an essential part of this process. *The Adult Faith Formation Library Series* offers a valuable collection of titles that are a reliable resource for formation, information, and transformation in the Catholic tradition.

The Series is perfect for

- Adults in a faith community who would like to grow through spiritual reading and reflection

- Parish/pastoral ministers who seek support in their personal and professional development

- Pastoral teams or school faculties who desire to enrich or further explore their mission

- Individuals who want to deepen their own understanding of the faith

Each volume's user-friendly format provides

- An introduction to the topic
- Four chapters, each designed for reading in one sitting/ session
- Questions for personal reflection and journaling, or for conversation starters in a team or learning community

Boston College's STM Online: Crossroads (**www.bc.edu/crossroads**) uses this series in its innovative course-style learning program. Crossroads gathers participants from the English-speaking world and creates learning communities that discuss the book together online. Pacing the conversation by using a chapter a week, a facilitator keeps the conversation going, encourages deeper discussion, and inquires how the reading inspires new or renewed spiritual practice. These popular courses are used as adult faith formation tools and as professional development experiences for ministers.

Whether used in formal educational settings or in less formal learning communities, *The Adult Faith Formation Library Series* offers faith formation in an accessible, flexible format for those who seek to live their faith in vibrant and informed ways in today's world.

CONTENTS

INTRODUCTION

I WROTE THIS VOLUME WITH TWO MAIN GOALS IN MIND: first, to introduce readers to four central themes of the Old Testament; and second, to explore these themes in the order of their appearance in the Bible. Thus, they become a way of tracing the biblical story itself. Of course, the themes overlap sometimes, but in general, the order of this book's chapters follows the biblical narrative as it unfolds from the Book of Genesis through the Book of Kings. Each chapter concludes with a brief section called "Looking Ahead," which discusses how each theme recurs in later parts of the Bible (e.g., the prophets, the wisdom books, and the New Testament). This purpose of this section is to show that these four themes are open-ended; they shaped the theological imaginations of later biblical writers, who adapted the themes to their own historical moment and their style of writing.

As I trace the biblical narrative in this book, I am especially interested in showing how the relationship between God and creation develops from Genesis to Kings. This focus is rooted in the teaching of the Vatican II document *Dei Verbum* (1965), which remains the Catholic Church's most authoritative teaching on Scripture. *Dei Verbum* stresses that Scripture is above all about fellowship—between God and the humans within Scripture, and between God and us who read Scripture (para 2). This fellowship, like all relationships, grows and changes. Biblical characters "came to know by experience the ways of God with men [and women]…and gained deeper and clearer understanding of His ways" (para 14). By learning about their deepening relationship with God, I hope that readers of this volume will become all the more attuned to God's dynamic presence in their lives.

ONE

CREATION

EVERYONE KNOWS THAT THE BIBLE BEGINS "IN THE BEGINNING." For Jews this phrase (Hebrew *bere'shit*) gives the Book of Genesis its title, since Jewish tradition names biblical books after their first word. No less important, however, is the second word of the Bible—"(he) created," or *bara'* in Hebrew. This word doesn't refer to any kind of creation but specifically denotes divine creation; God is the exclusive subject of this verb. Humans in the Bible can make, build, fashion, construct, etc., but only God can *bara'*. Between Genesis 1:1 and 2:4 the verb occurs seven times as God creates the heavens and earth, the creatures of sea, air, and land, and human beings. The use of this special verb at the beginning of the Bible and its repetition in subsequent verses makes an important point about divine agency in the Old Testament in general and creation in particular. God is not just a participant in this story but the featured actor. The story begins with an action that only God can perform.

Two Accounts of Creation

God's active participation continues as a defining feature of the creation stories. I write creation stories (plural) because scholars agree that Genesis 1—3 contains not one but two accounts of creation. The two stories are the beginnings of two distinct sources that course through the Pentateuch (the Bible's first five books). In the Bible as we know it today these (and other) threads have been woven together as a single narrative, but through careful study of Scripture, scholars have been able to identify particular threads in the final text. Although scholars disagree on the number of threads and their content, all agree that the Pentateuch is a composite text made up of various sources written by various authors at various times and places. "Source criticism" and the "Documentary Hypothesis" are often used as shorthand for the study of these different sources that comprise the final form of the Pentateuch.

As an analogy, imagine that you are compiling your family history based on journals that your grandparents left behind. Perhaps also a family member thought to interview them before they died, and you plan to include these testimonies in the family history you're developing. One approach to your project would be to compile these sources but keep each separate, or you could also choose to weave them into a single grand narrative. The Pentateuch is an example of the latter option; it is a compilation of different sources, which an editor has woven into an elegant and coherent story. (For a biblical example of the former approach, consider the four New Testament gospels, which tell the same story but remain distinct sources.) In addition to compiling sources, the editor of the Pentateuch also contributed original material. This writing includes stories as well as transitions between inherited sources. Scholars refer to this final editor as the Priestly writer(s) because of the prominence of priestly topics and vocabulary in his writing. Although scholars disagree on the number and content of the Pentateuch's various sources, nearly all agree that the Priestly writer was the editor who gave the sources their definitive shape and that this work was completed during the Babylonian Exile (586–539 BCE), a time when the Jews were expelled from their promised land.

Returning to the analogy of the family history project, imagine that you've compiled the various testimonies of your grandparents and you find that certain stories occur in the journals of more than one grandparent. Maybe these versions are identical, but more likely they disagree in certain details. Do you choose one account and dismiss the duplicates, or do you include more than one version of the same story? Do you harmonize discrepancies, or do you let each version stand as you received it? In both questions the editor chose the latter, preferring to preserve the plurality of traditions that had been handed down, even if such preservation resulted in inconsistencies and repetition within the final product. The existence of two creation stories in Genesis 1—3 is one example of this preservation.

Repetitions and discrepancies in the Bible may challenge our modern preference for seamless storytelling, but in no way do they undermine the integrity of the story it tells or the God it reveals. Indeed, these "rough edges" are no different than the challenges we confront in the gospels, which accent different parts of Jesus' story and sometimes disagree on details. The multiple sources of both the Pentateuch and the gospels are not competing accounts but witnesses of how particular communities were preserving and living out their sacred story. As in the hypothetical family history project, the preservation of multiple sources in the Pentateuch, even with their inconsistencies, is the best way to honor the diversity of sources that have come down. Their distinct versions of God's relationship with creation and with Israel are an advantage rather than a detriment, because their combination yields a theological tapestry that would be impossible to produce without a plurality of narrative threads.

Before looking at the creation accounts themselves, let's return one last time to our analogy of your family history and imagine sharing the final product with a close relative. Even though you have skillfully woven together your diverse sources, do you think a relative would be able to recognize particular voices within the narrative? Maybe your grandmother had certain phrases that she used often and are easily recognizable. Perhaps your grandfather was known to have strong opinions about this or that; when one of those opinions surfaces in a section, your relative can identify it with him. This kind of analysis has been the work of biblical scholars for more than a century. By noticing the distribution of certain vocabulary, motifs, and themes, scholars have attempted to identify the sources that comprise the Pentateuch. These efforts can benefit not only scholars but also people of faith. Although the principal interest of the faithful naturally lies in the final form of the text that we encounter in the Bible today and hear in liturgy, appreciation of the Pentateuch's different sources can bring to light its rich theological diversity. Hopefully, the following comparison of the Priestly creation story (Gen 1:1—2:4a) and the Garden of Eden story (Gen 2:4b—3:24) will demonstrate this richness.

The Priestly Creation Account

Although the Eden story was written *before* the Priestly creation story, the latter comes first in the canonical order. As the final editor of the Pentateuch, the Priestly writer was able to put his account first, as a way to introduce language, ideas, and motifs that run through the rest of the Pentateuch. Chief among these characteristics is the Priestly writer's transcendent view of God. In Genesis 1:1—2:4 we meet the God who creates the entire cosmos but does so *outside* the cosmos itself. If you were making a film of this creation story, God himself would be dictating the action from somewhere off-screen.

Further evidence of this transcendent view of God is the lack of anthropomorphic language. Other biblical texts refer to God's hand, arm, face, back, etc., but there are no such references in Genesis 1:1—2:4. Here, creation is accomplished through the power of God's spoken word coming from somewhere beyond creation itself. The only other mode of divine agency in this story is the "spirit (Heb. *ruah*) of God" that sweeps over the waters in 1:2, but this manifestation is likewise incorporeal. Such transcendence makes all the more radical God's decision to make human beings in God's own image (1:26–27). We will say more about these verses below, but here we can note a marvelous paradox: God exists far beyond us, but at the same time we are inextricably connected to him through our creation in his image.

Another key feature of the Priestly creation story is its emphasis on order, which is apparent in its content as well as style. Note, for example, the correspondence between Days 1–3 and Days 4–6; on the first three days God created generalities and environments, and the next three days feature the particularities of those environments. Thus on Day 1 he created light in general, and on Day 4 he made the sun, moon, and stars as specific manifestations of that light; on Day 2 God made the sky to separate the waters above and below, and on Day 5 he made the birds and sea creatures that inhabit the sky and waters; on Day 3 he made the dry land, and on Day 6 he created land animals and humans. This arrangement of the first six days shows that God's creation was no haphazard undertaking but a carefully ordered process that produced a carefully ordered universe. The structure also highlights the unique significance of the seventh day, which has no counterpart. God's "rest" (Heb. *shabat*, hence our word "Sabbath") on this day establishes a precedent that will later be prescribed for Israel (Exod 16:23; 20:8–11).

The Priestly writer's focus on order is reinforced by the style of Genesis 1:1—2:4, which features a formulaic, almost liturgical, rhythm. Each day follows the same basic pattern: announcement ("God said") → command ("Let there be…") → report ("And it was so") → evaluation ("And God saw that it was good") → temporal framework ("And there was evening and there was morning, the first day"). This literary structure is a good example of style matching content. Already we have observed the careful structure of the six days of creation, and now we can see how the formulaic style of Genesis 1:1—2:4a underscores this sense of order.

Such repetition makes all the more noteworthy those times when the author breaks the pattern. For example, there is one occasion when God amplifies his daily evaluation of creation by declaring the sixth day *very* good" (1:31). This boost was a subtle way for the author to indicate the special significance of humankind within God's creation. Similarly, the description of God's rest on the seventh day (2:1–3) breaks the formulaic style of the first six days, thus highlighting its uniqueness in creation and in the biblical week. The special status of the seventh day is made explicit when God declares it "holy," a word that in Hebrew means "set apart." Even before this declaration, however, we can infer its singularity by its departure from the daily pattern.

Other features of the Priestly creation story come into focus by comparing it to the creation accounts of Israel's neighbors in the ancient Near East, especially Babylon, where the Priestly author wrote and edited. After the Babylonian army destroyed Jerusalem in 586 BCE, they deported thousands of Jews to Babylon, where they lived until their release in 539 BCE. Despite this immense tragedy—or maybe because of it—the Babylonian Exile was a time of remarkable literary and theological creativity. On the one hand, it makes perfect sense that such tragedy would prompt Jews to consolidate their texts and traditions. On the other hand, however, it is astounding that, in the wake of devastating destruction, the Priestly writer could depict in Genesis 1:1—2:4 the God of Israel with such power, transcendence, and goodness. This historical background makes this theology of creation all the more inspiring and compelling.

The Babylonian setting of Genesis 1:1—2:4 is also important because in several places it is clear that the author has been influenced by creation accounts of the ancient Near East, particularly the Babylonian cosmology (i.e., story of the beginning of the cosmos) *Enuma elish*. Such influence is not surprising, since all writers, including biblical authors, are shaped by their social and cultural context. What makes the influence significant is not that Babylonian elements have been adopted but how the author has *adapted* them. For example, in Near Eastern tradition creation was the outcome of divine combat, or theomachy; deities battled, and the victor would use the body of the vanquished to create the cosmos. In the *Enuma elish* it is Marduk, the chief Babylonian god, who defeats Tiamat, the goddess of watery depths, and constructs the universe with her remains.

The opening verses of the Priestly creation story echo this tradition but put a biblical spin on it. In particular, the spirit of God sweeping over the deep in Genesis 1:2 seems to be a vestige of the divine battle that leads to creation. Key evidence of this interpretation is the Hebrew word *tehom*, usually translated "deep," which is cognate with the name Tiamat. According to this view, the author adopted the theomachy tradition but adapted it for a monotheistic context. There is still a divine victory over the forces of chaos, but this triumph is achieved not through a battle between deities but through the one God of Israel whose *ruaḥ* subdues the roiling deep.

This background underscores one of the most important features of Genesis 1:1—2:4, namely, that biblical creation was not the production of something out of nothing (*creatio ex nihilo*) but the transformation of a chaotic and inhospitable environment into an ordered one that supports life. In English translations this pre-creation chaos is called a "formless void," but the original Hebrew has a better ring to it: *tohu wa-bohu*. The biblical authors are not interested, as we might be, in what preceded this waterlogged wilderness or whence it came; what captured their theological imagination was not the origins of the *tohu wa-bohu* but the makeover it received from God. Thus biblical creation involves the organization of existing matter more than the manufacture of new things.

Note, for example, the prominence of the verb "to separate" in Genesis 1. Day and night are made by separating light from darkness (v. 4), and the sky is made by a dome that separates the waters above from the waters below (v. 7). (Israelites believed that the world was still surrounded by the primordial waters but were kept in check by the dome above and by pillars below. These waters only made their way to earth through subterranean springs or as precipitation released by God through windows in the dome [see Gen 7:11].) Similarly, the dry land is created by piling the leftover waters into seas (v. 10). What made God's creation marvelous was not his ability to make something from nothing but to transform a deadly wilderness into a life-giving cosmos.

There are two other places where the Babylonian context of Genesis 1 provides important background. First, when God creates the sun and moon in verse 16, it is easy to miss that neither is explicitly named; instead they are called the greater and the lesser lights. This language probably contains a subtle polemic against the Babylonian pantheon, which included a sun god and a moon god. By omitting their names and reducing them to nameless lamps, the author rejects their divine status and reiterates the singular transcendence of the God of Israel.

A more significant break from the Babylonian context in which the Priestly author was writing is the creation of humans in verses 26–28. Many are struck by the "us" in verse 26, but this plural pronoun would not have surprised ancient readers, who took for granted that God was surrounded by a council of subordinate deities (cf. 1 Kgs 22:19–22). Instead, the surprise for ancient readers would have been the conferral of God's image to all humankind. This view of humanity is quite different from Near Eastern cosmologies, like the *Enuma elish*, in which humans were created to provide for the needs of the gods so they could enjoy a life of divine leisure. If anyone received the divine image, it was the king, for whom it was a sign of divine authority. In Genesis 1, however, this honor is given to all humankind as part of their vocation of stewardship rather than subservience. This vocation is made explicit in verse 28, where humans are given dominion over the earth. In no way is this mandate permission for imprudent consumption and environmental degradation. Rather humans are expected to imitate the dominion of God in whose image they were made. The goodness, order, and harmony that define God's dominion over creation must be the hallmarks of human stewardship of the earth.

The Garden of Eden Story

Genesis 2:4 represents the turning point between the two creation accounts. This verse begins by summarizing the preceding story of "the heavens and the earth when they were created" and goes on to introduce the story of when "the LORD God made the earth and the heavens." Already in this verse we can observe an important shift: whereas the Priestly account refers to God simply as "God" (Heb. *Elohim*), the Eden story adds "Lord," which is the conventional translation of God's proper name *Yahweh*. Because Jewish law forbids the pronunciation of this name, which is considered too holy for human discourse, Jews usually substitute for it the Hebrew word *Adonai* ("lord"). This practice has been adopted by most translations of the Bible. Thus any time you encounter "Lord" in all caps (so as to distinguish it from non-divine instances of *adonai*), the word stands for God's holy name.

This shift to the name Yahweh is significant for several reasons. For one thing, the use of different divine names has been a key criterion for distinguishing the various sources of the Pentateuch. On a more theological level, however, the preference in the Eden story for the name Yahweh indicates a new perspective on God. Whereas in the Priestly account God was distant and transcendent, here God is depicted as down-to-earth and familiar. In addition to the use of God's personal name throughout the narrative, this theology is apparent in Yahweh's direct interactions with the first man and woman. Unlike the Priestly account, in which God creates through speech alone, in the Eden story he is literally hands-on: planting the garden, forming the man out of dust, putting him in the garden, removing his rib, and fashioning the woman. Later he talks and walks with the first couple. (For most of Genesis 2—3 the couple are not "Adam" and "Eve." She is not named until 3:20, and because Hebrew *adam* is the common word for "human," it is not always clear when the text is designating the man as a human in general or "Adam" in particular. He is often called "the *adam*," but by the end of the text "Adam" seems to be his proper name.)

The Eden story is so well known that its plot is familiar even to those who have never read the story. Such familiarity makes it hard to approach the story with fresh eyes, because we cannot read the text without importing the theologies that have been built on top of it. Nonetheless, the following analysis of the story attempts to read the story as a story and not as the basis for St. Paul's identification of Christ as the New Adam (Rom 5:12–21) or St. Augustine's doctrine of original sin. These and other interpretations of the Eden story are foundational to Christian belief, so setting them aside here is by no means a dismissal. Rather my goal is to offer a close reading of the ground floor of the text before it came to support these later theological edifices.

In this spirit I want to begin by emphasizing the artistry of the story itself. Some of this artistry is simple wordplay. The story contains many puns, such as the formation of the first human (*adam*) from earth (*adamah*), the drawing of woman (*ishah*) out of man (*ish*), and correlation between the snake's craftiness (*arum*) and the couple's nakedness (*arummim*). Another sign of literary sophistication is the story's dramatic irony. As readers, we know from the narrator more information than the man and woman in the story. For example, we know about the tree of life from 2:9, but God never mentions this tree to the couple (cf. 2:17); indeed, their expulsion from the garden is meant to ensure that they remain ignorant of it (3:22). Finally, the depiction of the snake is far more subtle than suggested by his post-biblical identification with Satan. His question to the woman in 3:1 is crafty because it distorts God's command from 2:16–17 just enough to sow doubt, and part of his prediction in 3:5 turns out to be true in 3:7. These literary features show the deft touch of the biblical author. The Eden story is not a one-dimensional morality play; it has inspired generations of Jews and Christians because it is a refined exploration of divine grace, human free will, and the consequences of disobedience.

Many readers wonder about the historical accuracy of the Eden story, and the short answer is that features of the story do not match what we know of the first humans. For example, God creates the man to till and keep the garden and later curses the soil that the man will work outside the garden (2:15; 3:17–18), but we know that humans lived as hunter-gatherers for two million years before they began cultivating crops in the Neolithic period (ca. 8000 BCE). Also noteworthy is the description of a man leaving his parents to join his wife (2:24), when other biblical texts depict the opposite (e.g., Gen 24:67). Such discrepancies are only a problem if we equate the story's truth with historical accuracy, but such an equation confuses the purpose of the Eden story. Ancient stories of origin were not meant to report history but to reveal the nature of God and humans. The truth of Genesis 2—3 lies in its compelling portrait of God, his relationship to the first man and woman, and the relationship between the man and the woman. Generations of Jews and Christians, including our own, have treasured the Eden story because they recognize themselves in the drama it depicts.

This drama revolves around the first couple's failure to comply with God's command to refrain from eating of the tree of knowledge of good and evil. Yahweh has furnished the garden with everything they could need, and all of it is available to them except this tree (and the tree of life). "Good and evil" could be an example of a merism, which uses two opposites to denote totality, like "young and old" or "high and low" in today's speech. If so, then "knowledge of good and evil" would be knowledge of everything. Alternatively, "good and evil" could refer to moral knowledge; eating the tree's fruit will expose the couple to moral complexity beyond their faculties. Lastly, it is important to note that "knowing" in the Bible is not just a cognitive process but also relational and experiential. To know in the Bible often implies intimate relationship, up to and including sexual intercourse, so "knowledge of good and evil" could signify experiential knowledge from which God would spare them.

Whichever meaning (or combination of them) we prefer, it is clear that the tree represents a level of knowledge for which God considers the man and woman unprepared. Their nakedness is an outward sign of their simplicity and naïveté. Yahweh even warns them that they will die when they eat the fruit, and at first this prediction seems to be false, especially compared to the snake's prognostication. The man and woman do not die, and their eyes are opened (3:4, 7). This strange outcome has been explained in various ways. Some have understood the couple's death in a spiritual rather than physical sense. The knowledge they received through their disobedience spoiled their perfect innocence; this loss is epitomized by the sudden awareness of their nudity. Another approach points out that God didn't mean the couple would die *immediately* after eating the fruit, since the Hebrew phrase translated "in the day" in 2:17 can mean more generally "when." Some who favor this reading assume that the couple was immortal while in the garden, and their disobedience led to their death insofar as they were expelled from the garden (but see 3:22).

My own preference draws on these interpretations but casts them in a more theological framework. Instead of thinking about the couple's existence in the garden in terms of physical immortality, we should see their life there as one of communion with Yahweh. In the garden the couple enjoyed the fullness of life that is only possible through encounter with God's presence, which leaves no room for death. Insofar as the couple's disobedience estranged them from God, the perfect life they experienced in his presence diminished. This is the "death" the man and woman suffer through their disobedience, and it has spiritual and physical consequences. Spiritually, their estrangement from God leads to fear and shame (3:10), and physically, their separation from God requires the couple to procreate. Offspring represented immortality in ancient Israel in that you lived on through your children and their children, but this afterlife only becomes necessary after the first couple's expulsion. There was no such thing as *after*life in the garden; the garden is life itself. Outside the garden, however, the man and woman must procreate to ensure their posterity. Procreation and all it entails, such as birth pangs and the woman's role as mother of all living ("Eve"), become necessary only after the couple's disobedience separates them from the fullness of life they once enjoyed in God's presence.

This interpretation brings us to the tragic irony at the center of the Eden story: through their desire to be closer to God, to share his knowledge, the first couple drove themselves away from him. The Eden story is filled with etiologies, i.e., explanations for why things are the way they are. By the end of this story we know why snakes slither on their belly, why women have pangs in childbirth, why farming is so toilsome, why men and women are drawn to each other, etc. But the story's most important and most poignant etiology explains why we are separated from the God who lovingly created us. It shows that the very quality that make humans preeminent among creation—their free will—alienates them from God insofar as it enables them to make choices contrary to the divine will. The Eden story is an attempt to reconcile, on the one hand, the belief in Yahweh, who provides abundant life and seeks relationship with humanity, and on the other hand, the separation we feel from God and the struggles that result from that estrangement. Even as the story mourns what has been lost and bemoans the difficulties of life outside the garden, it affirms the fundamental goodness of God and creation.

Compounding the first couple's alienation from God is their estrangement from each other. There is already a hint of trouble at the beginning of chapter 3, when the woman tells the snake what God has commanded. Her version adds a prohibition against even touching the tree's fruit (v. 3), which was not part of the original mandate given to the man before she had been created (2:17). What's more, the man never corrects her supplement or intervenes in her fruit-eating, even though he is with her throughout the scene (3:6). These details foreshadow larger problems to come. For example, when God confronts the man about his disobedience, he takes no responsibility but passes the buck to the woman; likewise, she passes the buck to the snake (3:12–13). We often focus on how the couple's disobedience separated them from Yahweh, but also significant is the division it exposes between them. There is no solidarity between them when their betrayal is exposed. Their estrangement culminates in God's declaration in 3:16 of enmity between the woman and the snake and inequality between her and the man, but this declaration is built on earlier disharmony in the story.

The subjugation of women to men in 3:16 presents a challenge to the more egalitarian sensibilities of modern readers. The challenge is formidable, but I offer here some points that may put the verse in a new light. First, although most modern Bibles read "he shall rule," the modality of this verb is ambiguous. Such modality is not explicit in Hebrew, so it is up to translators to supply the right helping verb. Most prefer "shall" here, but "may/could/can/might" would also be acceptable. (Compare Genesis 4:7, for example, which features a deliberate echo of 3:16, but in this verse the same verb is translated "you can/must master.") The point is that God's statement in 3:16 may not be a divine prescription of gender inequality but a *description* of potential discord, which, based on the couple's earlier blame game, seems all too likely. According to this interpretation, inequality between men and women is not so much a punishment as a consequence of their past behavior. God does not desire their disharmony any more than he desires for them to live apart from himself, but their choices have made both outcomes unavoidable.

An important assumption of this interpretation is that the first man and woman were created as equal partners in Eden. This equality is explicit in the Priestly story, in which male and female were simultaneously created in God's image (1:27), but this point has not always been appreciated in the Eden story. Some readers might suppose the woman's secondary creation indicates her diminished status, but in the story her creation follows a series of unsuitable partners for the man. Only when Yahweh forms woman out of the same flesh and bone does he create a true partner (2:23). In this way her secondary creation actually highlights her complementary equality; her perfection is apparent in light of the preceding failures.

Others have regarded her designation as "help(er)" (2:18) as another belittlement, but this reading is refuted by the frequent use of this word as a divine epithet, especially in the Psalms. If the psalmist praises God by calling him "my help(er)" (Pss 33:20; 70:5; 115:9–11; 146:5), then it is hard to read the same word in Genesis as a slight against the woman. Finally, many suppose that the act of naming in the Bible implies the power to define who or what is named, but the evidence for this meaning is thin. Most often, naming in the Bible is a sign of discernment rather than definition; a name describes, not prescribes, an essential feature of a person or thing. Thus God calls Jacob "Israel" *after* he has "striven"

(Gen 32:28). This naming cannot indicate control because Jacob is the one who prevailed; similarly, no one would suppose that Hagar has subordinated Yahweh when she names him "God-of-my-seeing" (Gen 16:13). Thus the man (*ish*) calls the woman *ishah* (2:23) because he recognizes their common substance, and later he calls her Eve ("life"), once he realizes that she will be "the mother of all living" (3:20). The name comes at the end of the narrative because that is when her unique role in procreation has become apparent. The point of these reflections is to show that the inequality announced by God in 3:16 was not part of God's original plan; rather the couple was created for the purpose of mutual support and solidarity. God's announcement simply names the discord that the man and woman have themselves demonstrated.

There are several other important points to make about the punishments recorded in 3:14–19. First, we must be careful not to call them all curses. In fact, only the snake and the ground are cursed (vv. 14, 17). Unlike contemporary use of curse words, curses in the ancient world were solemn, binding, and not taken lightly. For this reason the lack of explicit curse language for the man and the woman is significant. Despite their disobedience Yahweh shows mercy in sparing them the irrevocable punishment he imposes on the snake and ground. The couple is not completely exempt—after all, humanity (*adam*) has been formed from the now-cursed ground (*adamah*)—but Yahweh's forbearance leaves open the possibility of renewed relationship with him. In fact, as I suggested above, God's punishments for the couple may more rightly be called consequences. Their choices have made it impossible to stay in the garden, and 3:16–19 describes the "new normal" outside of Eden, which includes interpersonal strife, procreation, and agricultural hardship. But none of these new realities are sworn as curses, and if human choices have resulted in these difficulties, then it is possible that different choices can lead to their attenuation. This possibility is indicated by Yahweh himself when, just before the couple's expulsion, he provides them with sturdy leather garments to replace their flimsy fig leaves (3:21). The first man and woman must accept the consequences of their disobedience, but God does not doom them to fail. Divine mercy exceeds justice as God prepares them for life apart from the fullness of his life-giving presence.

Looking Ahead

Although Genesis 1–3 contains two creation stories written by different authors, they agree on certain key features of creation. These commonalities include God's loving transformation of an inhospitable environment into a "good" one in which life flourishes; the foremost status of humankind in creation, its unique relationship with God, and its role as steward of God's creation; and a strong interest in safeguarding the ordered harmony of creation, especially maintaining the boundary between the divine and human realms. In particular, the stories raise the question of how God and humankind can be in relationship in a way that honors their unique connection but also upholds the boundary between them.

This question will animate much of the remaining chapters of Genesis as God tries to find the right way to be in relationship with the humans he has made in his image. In fact, as we shall see in the next chapter on covenant, this question continues beyond Genesis and even into the New Testament. However, the question of divine-human relations is especially acute in the Primeval History (i.e., Genesis 1—11), which describes God's earliest interactions with humankind. These chapters depict a kind of "trial and error," as God seeks relationship with humanity but is frustrated by their failure to maintain the boundaries he has established. These episodes are relevant to our discussion of creation because they address similar issues and, as we will see, employ some of the same imagery.

The story of Noah and the flood is a prime example of the continuing aftermath of the creation stories. It begins with clear violations of God's created order, as divine beings are procreating with human women (6:1–4) and the earth was filled with violence (6:11). Although "violence" suggests physical harm, the word in Hebrew can also mean distortion, as when we say that something "does violence" to a text. This latter meaning implies the corruption of the created order, which humans were tasked to maintain. This travesty grieves God; he regrets his creation of humans and decides to start over (6:6–7). Indeed, the flood is simply a reversal of the creative process described in Genesis 1. There God separated the waters above and below so that habitable dry land could emerge, and here he allows those waters to cover the earth again. Even the *tehom*, whose subjugation by God's *ruaḥ* was the first step of creation, returns as a symbol of the world's return to its primordial state of chaos (6:11).

Just as the flood is a divine act of un-creation, the recession of the waters should be seen as a re-creation. Once again the process begins with God's *ruaḥ* blowing forth, and once again the primordial waters, including the *tehom*, are separated so that dry land can emerge again (Gen 8:1–5). After the ark comes to rest, the animals are "brought forth" just as God "brought them forth" in the beginning (Gen 1:24; 8:17), and God commands Noah to "be fruitful and multiply" just as he commanded the first human (Gen 1:28; 9:1). This analysis of the flood story shows that creation is not a one-off divine action that takes place only "in the beginning" but one that God performs again (and again).

Indeed, it is hard to overstate the importance of creation in the theological imagination of the biblical writers. It is a theme that recurs throughout the Bible. For example, although the Exodus story in many ways represents a new chapter in God's relationship with creation through the election of Israel, this story of redemption draws on the language and imagery of creation. In particular, the most dramatic part of the Exodus story, the crossing of the Red Sea, involves a blast of God's *ruah*, the separation of waters, and the emergence of dry ground (Exod 14:21–22, 29; 15:8). The difference is the final result of this divine action; here it produces a people (Exod 15:16) instead of the cosmos. The Exodus is rightly regarded as Israel's national story of redemption, but it is important to recognize that God's intervention in the story repeats the saving action he performed at creation. Just as God's creation of a life-giving world out of the *tohu wa-bohu* was a kind of redemption, so is God's redemption of Israel a kind of creation.

Creation imagery occurs throughout the Psalter as well. Psalm 8, for example, is a hymn to creation that expresses wonder at the magnificence of God's handiwork. The psalmist's contemplation of creation leads to the famous question: What are human beings that you are mindful of them (8:4)? Such a question would be equally at home in Genesis 1, where we marvel at God's transcendent power in creation alongside his decision to make humankind in his image. In other psalms we find the descriptions of the theomachy that is often associated with creation, but unlike Genesis 1, this divine combat has not been demythologized. Instead we find in Psalm 74 Yahweh vanquishing Leviathan and other sea monsters as a prelude to his creation of day, night, the sun, earth, and seasons (vv. 12–17), and in Psalm 89 he crushes Sea and Rahab before founding the world and all that is in it (vv. 9–13). Significantly, neither psalm is a creation hymn *per se*; Psalm 74 is a communal lament, and Psalm 89 is a royal psalm-turned-communal lament. These psalms show that creation imagery was part of the theological repertoire that could be enlisted in various contexts. Here the psalmist's community celebrates God's creative power in the hope that he will bring that power to bear in their present crisis.

Such an appeal to God's creative power is also found in the prophetic books of the Bible, especially the Book of Isaiah. Like Genesis 1, chapters 40—55 of Isaiah (usually called "Second Isaiah") were written during the Babylonian Exile and depict creation as the ultimate sign of Yahweh's cosmic supremacy. The prophet uses creation to inspire hope in the Jewish exiles that Yahweh can and will transform their catastrophe into new life. After asking the exiles, "Who has directed the spirit (*ruaḥ*) of the LORD" (40:13), Second Isaiah directs their gaze to the heavens and asks: "Who created (*bara'*) these?" The answer is God who "call[s] them all by name; because he is great in strength, mighty in power, not one is missing" (40:26). The prophet continues: "Have you not known? Have you not heard? The LORD is the everlasting God, the Creator (*bara'*) of the ends of the earth" (40:28). Like the Priestly writer and the psalmist, Second Isaiah uses the language and imagery of creation to bring hope to people in crisis.

Finally, examples from wisdom literature also attest to the enduring significance of creation in the Old Testament. The Book of Proverbs includes several speeches by personified Wisdom in which she associates herself with creation. She claims to have been the first of Yahweh's creations, who then played a role in his creative work (8:22–31). When he established the heavens, circumscribed the deep (*tehom*), and fixed the earth's foundations, she "was beside him, like a master worker." Unlike Second Isaiah and Psalms 74 and 89, Proverbs does not use creation imagery to inspire hope in the midst of crisis but to reveal Wisdom as the organizing principle of the cosmos. Wisdom's role in creation should convince the audience of Proverbs that their pursuit of her is a way to participate in God's plan for all of creation. In fact, in a startling reinterpretation of the Eden story, Wisdom is called the "tree of life" whom we should seek as the way to long life and prosperity (Prov 3:13–18). Far from barring access to the tree of life and its immortality (Gen 3:22, 24), Proverbs encourages its audience to lay hold of it.

All of these examples of creation beyond the Book of Genesis show the prominence of this theme in the theological imagination of the biblical writers. Creation is not something God does only at the beginning of the Bible but is an essential part of his ongoing interaction with the world.

Questions *for* Reflection

How do the two creation stories in Genesis 1—3 combine to give us a fuller picture of God that would be unbalanced with just one or the other?

How can the biblical understanding of creation as God's ongoing transformation of chaos into life-sustaining order enrich other areas of theological reflection? For example, what are its implications for our spiritual lives? For environmental ethics?

How does God's sometimes rocky partnership with humanity in Genesis 1—11 resonate with our own relationship with God?

TWO

COVENANT

This chapter explores the theme of covenant in the Old Testament, and it picks up where the previous chapter left off. There we concluded with a brief discussion of the flood story in Genesis 6—9 as a process of un-creation and re-creation, and this same story opens the present chapter because it contains the first example of covenant in the Bible. Although we may be tempted to think of Yahweh's special relationship with Adam and Eve as covenantal, in fact the Hebrew word for covenant *berit* does not occur in the Eden story, and its absence is significant. God's covenant is not established at creation but emerges later as a solution to a stubborn question, namely, how can God and humanity be in a relationship that bears out their unique affinity but also maintains a proper boundary between them?

This question was introduced last chapter, and it is one that persists from Eden through the generations leading up to Noah (and beyond). The transgression of the divine-human boundary lies at the heart of the Eden debacle and also the flood story. In the former the first humans' desire to be like God leads to their disobedience and expulsion (Gen 3:5, 22), and in the latter procreation between divine and human beings leads to God's cathartic flood (Gen 6:1–4). After these calamities God tries a new approach with Noah and his family; he will enter into a more formal relationship with his creation. The biblical term for this formal relationship is Hebrew *berit*, which is translated "covenant" but literally means "something between." A *berit* is a contract "between" two partners in which one or both commit by sworn oath to fulfill certain obligations. There are numerous covenants in the Old Testament, including contracts between two human partners (e.g., Gen 21:27; 31:44), but this chapter will focus on divine covenants, in particular, the Noahide covenant (Gen 9:8–17), the Abrahamic covenant (Gen 15, 17), and the Sinai covenant (Exod 19—24). We will conclude the chapter with some remarks on the reinterpretation of these covenants in later books, especially the Old Testament prophets and the New Testament gospels. God's covenant with David will be discussed at length in chapter 4, which will look at kingship in the Old Testament.

Before exploring these particular examples of covenant, however, it will be worthwhile to discuss further the concept itself. I mentioned above that covenant should be understood as God's solution to the challenge of negotiating the divine-human relationship. The advantage of this understanding is its illumination of certain literary and theological features of covenant. Literarily, it restores some suspense to the biblical narrative. Sometimes biblical stories seem so familiar, we let our knowledge of their ending obscure the literary artistry that leads us there. But if we suspend our knowledge of the covenants to come and follow the story as it unfolds, we gain a new appreciation for the conundrum driving the biblical narrative. Here is an all-powerful God who loves humans so much that he has made them in his image and given them free will to make their own choices, even ones that are contrary to his will and their best interests. How can God be in relationship with these independent creatures without compromising his sovereignty or diminishing their free will? (Parents may empathize with this difficulty in that they too are faced with the challenge of honoring their children's independence without surrendering their responsibility for the children's safety and prosperity.)

Against this backdrop we can recognize the novelty of God's covenant through Noah in Genesis 9. After several false starts, God has found a new way to relate to creation, and we wonder if this new approach will at last be successful. Alas, it is not! Soon the humans are building the Tower of Babel, which they hope will bring them into the divine realm (Gen 11:4). Yahweh responds by revising the covenantal approach; instead of establishing a covenant with all of creation, he will enter a covenant with a single person—Abra(ha)m—through whom he will extend his blessing to the rest of the world. The covenant at Sinai is yet another development in this unfolding relationship between Yahweh and his people. Covenants are not one-size-fits-all; human societies change, and those changes require God to find new ways to relate to creation. Israel after the Exodus is not the same people they were before their sojourn in Egypt, and those differences are reflected in the Sinai covenant. Covenants are a way for Yahweh to meet his people where they are at various stages in their history; they are milestones in a relationship that unfolds across both testaments.

Theologically, this perspective helps us appreciate the poignant urgency of God's love for creation and the divine hope expressed in the covenants he establishes. True relationship involves vulnerability on both sides, and this is no less true for the divine-human relationship. The free will given by God makes it possible for him to be wounded by human sin, as we learn at the beginning of the flood story when the narrator tells us that Yahweh "was sorry that he had made humankind on the earth, and it grieved him to his heart" (Gen 6:6). This regret leads to the near extinction of humankind in the flood, but the covenant at the end of the story reasserts God's hope for the future of humankind. The covenant reveals God's willingness to find new ways of being in relationship with the creation he loves, and the subsequent covenants show God's attentiveness to the changing needs of his people.

One way to think about biblical covenant is to compare it to a contractual relationship in our own day, namely, marriage. In the beginning stages of a relationship, there is no need for a formal arrangement, as two people get to know each other. As the relationship grows in intimacy, however, it becomes more necessary for the partners to express their expectations of each other (e.g., dating exclusively, making important life decisions together), and the couple may finally decide to formalize their relationship with marriage. Likewise, biblical covenants may be read as formal bonds that punctuate the courtship that takes place throughout Genesis and Exodus. In these books God is getting to know these humans whose free will makes them unpredictable even to him, and he too is revealing more of himself to Israel, especially in Exodus. There God explains that the goal of his actions is that Israel "will know that I am Yahweh" (Exod 6:7; 7:17; 10:2; 16:6; etc.), and he makes known to Moses and Israel the divine name Yahweh, which he withheld from Abraham, Isaac, and Jacob (Exod 3:13–15; 6:2–3). The key word in these examples is the verb "to know," which in Hebrew means more than cognition; it implies intimate relationship, sometimes even sexual relations (cf. our expression "to know in the biblical sense"). Thus biblical covenants resemble marriage in that they formalize the commitment of God and Israel to each other after an engagement of growing intimacy.

The Noahide Covenant (Genesis 9)

Although the covenant at the end of the flood story is often called the Noahide covenant, it pertains not only to Noah but also to his descendants and even to all creatures of the earth (9:9–10). This universal scope provides the backdrop for the more particular covenants that follow. These subsequent covenants focus on one family (Abraham's), one people (Israel), or one person (the Davidic king), but none of them abrogate the universalism of the Noahide covenant. Although Israel will come to play a unique role the divine plan as God's "treasured possession" and a "holy nation" (Exod 19:5–6), Israel's election is part of God's larger plan for all of creation. Indeed, the Noahide covenant holds a special place in Jewish tradition as the foremost expression of God's love for all humankind. Humans are expected to reciprocate this love by fulfilling seven commandments, one of which is the prohibition in Genesis 9:4 of eating a living animal. This tradition demonstrates the importance Jews have placed on the Noahide covenant and its universal scope.

In the biblical text itself there is only one obligation placed on Noah and his descendants, and it actually occurs before the covenant itself. In 9:3–6 God permits Noah to eat animals but requires that the animals' blood be drained before they are prepared for eating. This practice, which is a requirement for kosher meat today, is based on the belief that blood is the life-force of creatures (see Lev 17:11), and it represents a significant shift from the eating habits of earlier generations. According to Genesis 1:28–30 the first humans and animals had the same diet of plants and fruits, but now in 9:1–4 God establishes a food chain between them. It seems that the violence of recent generations has taught God something about humans' propensity for bloodshed, and he is willing to concede a carnivorous diet if it will forestall the shedding of human blood. After all, the desires of the human heart are no less evil after the flood than they were before the flood (8:21). As we noted in the introduction to this chapter, covenants should be read as examples of God finding new ways to enter in relationship with humankind. In order to avoid repeating the destruction brought about by human wickedness, God revises the order of his creation to foster a more peaceful existence.

Alas, this harmony does not extend to animals, who are now subject to the carnivorous appetite of humans, and that is not the only bad news for animals in Genesis 9. In verses 1–2 God repeats to Noah the command to be fruitful and multiply, but instead of going on to reaffirm humans' dominion over creation, as we find in the original command from Genesis 1:28, God tells Noah that the animals of the earth will live in fear and dread of humans. Although animals have been subordinated to humans from the beginning—it is humankind that is made in God's image and entrusted with the stewardship of God's creation—the creation stories presume a harmonious bond among all creatures. In the postdiluvian world, however, the distinction between humans and animals has been amplified, and God has renewed his relationship with humankind at the expense of the animals.

But that is not quite the whole story. For when we turn to the Noahide covenant itself, we find that the covenantal relationship includes not only Noah and his descendants but also "every living creature that is with you, the birds, the domestic animals, and every animal of the earth with you, as many as came out of the ark" (9:9–10). No other covenant in the Bible involves the animal kingdom so explicitly, and their inclusion provides an important counterbalance to animals' subordination in the verses leading up to the covenant. After giving Noah explicit instructions to ensure the survival of all species after the flood, God establishes with them the same bond he makes with Noah and his descendants. Thus the Noahide covenant is unique for its expansiveness; it creates a formal relationship between God and the children of Noah (i.e., all humankind) as well as between God and animals. Although God's inclusion of all creatures must be held in tension with the sharper distinction he draws between humans and animals, the Noahide covenant is an extraordinary expression of divine care for all of creation. Moreover, it represents an important step in God's developing relationship with creation as he recalibrates his expectations of humankind and finds new ways to engage the world he has created.

God also is implicated in this recalibration, since covenants involve commitments by both parties. Having commanded humans to refrain from shedding human blood and to consume animals in a prescribed way, God pledges never to cut off living beings with a destructive flood (8:21; 9:11). This promise underscores the theological point made in this chapter's introduction, namely, that the relationality intrinsic to covenants entails divine vulnerability. Of course, God is all-powerful and doesn't need to make any promises to the living beings he has created, but in the interests of establishing a covenantal relationship with his beloved creation, he *chooses* to put limits on his divine freedom. Knowing full well that humans' propensity for wrongdoing is still there (see 8:21), God promises to abstain from repeating the divine act of destruction he has just completed. Relationships require mutual commitments, and divine covenants are no exception. God's preference for a more intimate bond with his creatures over absolute divine freedom reveals his love for us and his desire to be with us.

Finally, we cannot talk about the Noahide covenant without discussing its most famous feature, namely, the rainbow that is given in 9:13 as a sign of the covenant. Such signs are a visible reminder to both parties of the agreement that has been reached between them, and they are a regular component of Pentateuchal covenants. As we shall see, circumcision is the sign of God's covenant with Abraham (Gen 17:11), and the Sabbath is the sign of God's covenant with Israel at Sinai (Exod 31:13). In this way the Priestly writers who were the final editors of the Pentateuch used covenantal signs as a structuring device for the books of Genesis and Exodus. The signs highlight the progressive covenants that punctuate the biblical narrative, but the differences among the signs reflect changes that take place within that progression. For example, insofar as a rainbow is a phenomenon that can be observed by anyone on earth, it is an apt sign for the Noahide covenant that God has established with all living beings. Circumcision and the Sabbath, by contrast, are more particular signs that correspond to more particularistic covenants. Although each sign is meant to be a reminder to both partners, God's comments on the rainbow emphasize its role in reminding him of his obligation to refrain from another flood. The emphasis points up again the willingness of God to place limitations on his own power if it means creating a more intimate bond with his creatures.

The Abrahamic Covenant (Genesis 15 and 17)

As noted in the introduction to this chapter, the Noahide covenant ends with the hope that God has found the right recipe for relationship with humankind, one that will celebrate their affinity but also honor the boundaries between their respective realms. Just one chapter later, however, we find humans again aspiring to make God's place their own. They hope to make a name for themselves with a tower whose top will reach the heavens (Gen 11:4). Yahweh frustrates their plans by multiplying their languages and scattering the people across the earth, but this dispersal contains the seed of a new beginning. For among these displaced families is Abram (later Abraham), the man whom God elects for yet another approach to humankind (11:31). Instead of entering into a covenantal relationship with all living beings, Yahweh will establish a covenant with one particular family and, through that family, extend his divine blessing to all the world.

God's relationship with Abram does not begin with covenant but with divine promises. In Genesis 12, after instructing Abram to leave his home and set out to a new place, Yahweh promises Abram three things: descendants, blessing, and land (vv. 2–3, 7). These promises, which will later be cemented in the formal covenant between Yahweh and Abram, are foundational for the rest of the Hebrew Bible. After all, the descendants of Abram are none other than people of Israel whose national story comprises the Old Testament narrative; the blessing that Abram receives is one that will extend to "all the families of the earth" (v. 3); and the land God promises him is the so-called Promised Land. At least one of these promises is implicated in every biblical story that follows the Abrahamic covenant.

A striking feature of this beginning of Yahweh's relationship with Abram is the lack of any explanation for the choice of Abram. Unlike Noah, whose selection to survive the flood was correlated to his righteousness (Gen 6:9), Abram is described with no characteristics indicating his worthiness for the promises he receives. Of course, he will later show himself to be worthy of them (Gen 15:6), but in Genesis 12 his election is portrayed as an act of divine grace. This aspect of Abram's call will recur throughout the Hebrew Bible as God calls forth leaders (judges, prophets, kings) for God's own reasons, often surprising those who have been selected (Exod 3:11; 4:10, 13; Judg 6:15; 1 Sam 9:21; 16:7; Isa 6:5; Jer 1:6). Like Abram's call, these vocation stories emphasize God's grace rather than the person's merit. God's agents are not chosen for their worthiness but are empowered by God to become worthy of the role to which God has called them.

The Abrahamic covenant itself is an example of a doublet, that is, a story that preserved in two different pentateuchal sources, both of which are recounted in the biblical narrative. The first version in Genesis 15 has been attributed to the Yahwist (J) source, and the second in Genesis 17 has been attributed to the Priestly (P) source. The former begins with Abram expressing impatience over the delay in the fulfillment of God's promises (15:2–3). God responds to his complaint by reiterating the promises, but then he takes this assurance one step further by entering into a covenant with Abram and thereby committing himself to their fulfillment.

The covenant is ratified in verses 9–10 and 17 by a ritual that is modeled after the ceremony that would conclude a treaty between two kingdoms in the ancient Near East. Like the ritual described in Genesis 15, the treaty ceremony consisted of bisecting animals and passing through their carcasses. This ceremony was prevalent enough in ancient Israel that it is reflected in the biblical expression for covenant-making; in Hebrew one "cuts" a covenant (e.g., Gen 15:18; Exod 24:8; 34:10). Moreover, we know from ancient treaty documents (and also from Jer 34:18–19) that the ritual signified a self-curse, i.e., whoever passed through the carcasses was committing himself to the same fate as the animals, should he violate the treaty. When treaties involved unequal partners, as was often the case, the weaker kingdom was the one to make perform this self-curse. (Adopting medieval terminology, scholars often refer to the stronger and weaker kingdoms as suzerains and vassals, respectively.) What makes Genesis 15 extraordinary is that it is not Abram but Yahweh, in the form of a flaming torch and firepot, who passes through the bisected animals (15:17). The God of Israel is so invested in the relationship he has cultivated with Abram and so committed to the promises he has made to him that he invokes the self-curse on himself. It is an astonishing example of divine vulnerability in the interest of covenantal intimacy.

Another ancient Near Eastern practice that may shed light on the Abrahamic covenant is the custom of land grants, which masters would bestow on loyal servants. Unlike the treaties, which emphasized the vassal's obligations toward the suzerain, the land grant expressed a master's obligation toward a servant. In particular, the master was obliged to give the servant land as a reward for his loyalty. Some scholars have compared the Abrahamic covenant to this land grant for several reasons. For one thing, the covenant is in fact a land grant; it confirms the promise of land that Yahweh made to Abram in chapter 12. Also, in contrast to treaties, which induced the future loyalty of a vassal through conditional rewards, both the land grant and the Abrahamic covenant convey unconditional promises that repay past loyalty. The advantage of this comparison is the way that it highlights the unconditional and promissory style of the Abrahamic covenant. It comes after the faith that Abram has already shown in Yahweh (15:6), and although God certainly expects Abram to continue his faithful allegiance, the divine promises are not contingent on it. By contrast, when we come to the Sinai covenant below, we will find that its form and explicitly conditional style make it a closer parallel to the treaty model.

The Priestly version of the Abrahamic covenant is recounted in Genesis 17. As a doublet of the J version, it repeats the main idea of the story (i.e., God makes a covenant with Abram), but the Priestly account should not be considered redundant. Rather it advances the narrative in important ways and offers new theological insights. For example, Genesis 17 is the first time that Sarai (soon to be Sarah) is explicitly named as the mother of the covenanted descendants of Abram. Up to this point that maternal role was unclear, especially in the preceding chapter, 16, which detailed Sarai's struggles to conceive and her harsh treatment of her slave and surrogate Hagar. Finally, this ambiguity is resolved in the Priestly version of the Abrahamic covenant, in which Sarai has her named changed to Sarah just as Abram's is changed to Abraham, and she is designated the mother of Abraham's promised heir and the recipient of divine blessing (17:15–16).

Another important feature of Genesis 17 is the way it builds on earlier themes in the Priestly narrative. God's promise to make Abraham exceedingly "numerous" and "fruitful" (vv. 2, 6) echo the command God gave to the first male and female in the Priestly creation story when he told them to "be fruitful and multiply" (Gen 1:28), and both verbs occur again when God gives the same command to Noah (Gen 9:1, 7). The repetition of these verbs in the Abrahamic covenant establishes continuity within the biblical narrative and shows God's commitment to the plan he set forth at creation.

Likewise, the institution of circumcision as a sign of the Abrahamic covenant (Gen 17:11) links it to the Noahide covenant, which also had a sign. The practice of circumcision among Jews can be traced back to this covenantal sign. As an outward sign that distinguishes Israel from Gentiles, circumcision is an apt symbol of the narrower scope of the Abrahamic covenant.

The divine blessing will still reach all the families of the earth who have been scattered from the Tower of Babel but will be mediated through God's covenant with Abraham in particular. Although circumcision might seem to be a requirement of the covenant, it is not a condition like the stipulations of the Sinai covenant. Rather, it is a badge of covenantal membership (cf. Exod 12:48), not unlike a wedding ring is an outward sign of membership in a marriage covenant. God's covenantal promises to Israel do not depend on the practice of circumcision any more than a marriage depends on a wedding ring; I am no less married when I take mine off while swimming. But Israelites who abstain from circumcision forgo the symbol that indicates their place in the covenantal community. This view of circumcision is important for our reading of Genesis 17 and also something to keep in mind when reading Paul's remarks on circumcision in the New Testament (1 Cor 7:19; Gal 6:11–15).

The Sinai Covenant (Exodus 19—24)

As noted in this chapter's introduction, the first half of the Book of Exodus can be read as a courtship between Israel and Yahweh. Assuring the Israelites that he remembers the promises he made to Abraham, Isaac, and Jacob (Exod 2:24; 6:8), Yahweh acquaints his people with his power and reveals himself in new ways to them. In particular, he makes known his holy name, Yahweh, in Exodus 3:15 and 6:3, and according to the latter verse, God had withheld this special name even from the patriarchs (though other Pentateuchal sources have been using the name Yahweh all along). This courtship builds to Exodus 19 when the Israelites arrive at Mount Sinai and Yahweh offers to enter into a special covenant with them. He reminds them what he has already done for them (v. 4) and then proposes that, if they will agree to obey his command and keep the covenant, he will exalt them even further. They will become a "treasured possession…a priestly kingdom and a holy nation" (vv. 5–6). Moses reports this offer to the people, who agree to everything that Yahweh has spoken (v. 8). This exchange is the foundation of the Sinai covenant; everything after this chapter builds on the basic equation that Israel will be Yahweh's people and Yahweh will be their God (v. 5; cf. 6:7). The formula echoes throughout the Old Testament, especially in the prophetic books (Jer 7:23; 11:4; 24:7; 30:22; 31:1, 33; 32:38; Ezek 11:20; 14:11; 34:30; 36:28; 37:23; Zech 8:8; 13:9).

Before looking at the covenant itself, we should note that God's request for Israel's obedience comes *after* he has rescued them from Egypt. He does not make their deliverance from oppression contingent on covenantal obligations but saves them with no guarantee of their later loyalty. Only after they have escaped the harsh life they endured in Egypt does God invite them into a deeper relationship with him. He has brought them to a place where they can make a free choice about their future with him. In theory, Israel could have declined Yahweh's offer and tried their chances with another deity, but they said yes. Before even knowing the exact commandments, the Israelites trusted what they knew of Yahweh's justice, power, and compassion and agreed to whatever covenantal obligations he would set before them.

These obligations are set forth in the Ten Commandments (Exod 20:1–17) and the Covenant Code (Exod 20:22—23:19) and are ratified in a covenant ceremony described in Exodus 24:1–11. Even more than the Abrahamic covenant described in Genesis 15, the Sinai covenant bears a strong resemblance to ancient Near Eastern suzerainty treaties. These treaties, which obliged a stronger kingdom (the suzerain) to protect a weaker kingdom (the vassal) in exchange for exclusive loyalty, followed a standard pattern that is reflected in the Sinai covenant. The pattern included 1) identification of the suzerain; 2) history of its relationship with the vassal; 3) stipulations imposed on the vassal; 4) deposition of treaty copies in temples; 5) invocation of gods as witnesses; and 6) list of blessings and curses according to the vassal's observance or violation of the treaty.

Many of these elements are found in the Sinai covenant. For example, the first of the Ten Commandments identifies Yahweh as the suzerain and recounts his history with his vassal Israel, and the remaining commandments represent the stipulations incumbent on Israel. Those are the only three elements of the treaty model found in Exodus 20, but elsewhere in the Pentateuch we find references to the deposition of treaty copies (Deut 10:1–5), the invocation of divine witnesses (Deut 4:26; 30:19; 31:28; 32:1), and lists of blessings and curses (Lev 26; Deut 27—28). Altogether these treaty parallels give us insight into the theological perspective of the biblical writers. Their use of the suzerainty treaty model indicates that they saw Israel as a weak kingdom that could depend on Yahweh for protection and well-being as long as they were loyal to their divine suzerain.

A key difference between the Sinai covenant and the previous covenants is its conditionality. This aspect of the Sinai covenant is encapsulated in the tiny English word "if." Note its use at the beginning of Exodus 19:5: "*If* you obey my voice and keep my covenant, you shall be my treasured possession out of all the peoples," and it is a regular feature in the Book of Deuteronomy (7:12 et al.). This contingency marks an important shift in the development of Yahweh's covenantal relationship with Israel. His covenantal promises to Abraham did not depend on Abraham's actions; they were simply given to him and his descendants with no strings attached. With the Sinai covenant we have entered a new phase of this relationship. Just as Yahweh has revealed more of himself to Moses and the Israelites, he expects more of the Israelites in the maintenance of their covenantal relationship.

The shared covenantal obligations of both God and Israel find expression in the Hebrew word *ḥesed*. Usually translated "loving kindness" or "steadfast love," the word denotes the mutual loyalty between two covenant partners, including between two human partners (e.g., Ruth 1:8; 3:10). The word implies relationship and reciprocity; *ḥesed* cannot be one-sided. In the Sinai covenant, *ḥesed* expresses God's enduring fidelity to Israel, even forgiving transgressions for the sake of their relationship (Exod 20:6; 34:6–7). Israel is expected to reciprocate this fidelity, and although this expectation is not expressed with the word *ḥesed* in the Book of Exodus, it is used by several prophets to call Israel back to covenantal fidelity (Hos 2:21; 6:6; Mic 6:8).

More concretely, Israel's covenantal obligations are expressed in the pentateuchal law codes. Besides the Ten Commandments, which we will discuss below, there are three main law codes in the Old Testament: the Covenant Code (Exod 20:22—23:33), the Holiness Code (Lev 17—26), and the Deuteronomic Code (Deut 12—26). Sometimes this legal material is dismissed by modern readers, not least Christians, as arcane and pedantic, and the theological reflex of this attitude has been to regard "the God of the Old Testament" (as if he were a separate deity) as nit-picky and legalistic. This view fails to appreciate biblical law as a profound gift that expresses God's love for his people and desire for them to flourish in an ordered society. Reciprocally, the laws give Israelites a way to show their *ḥesed* to Yahweh and solidarity with each other. In this way, covenantal law is just as much a sign of Yahweh's love and justice as his liberation of Hebrew slaves from their bondage in Egypt. Both reveal his commitment to Israel's well-being and invite Israel to respond in service to God and each other.

Within the larger tradition of the Sinai covenant, the Ten Commandments in Exodus 20 have long held a special significance in Jewish and Christian tradition. These commandments, or "words" as they are called in the biblical text (v. 1; cf. "Decalogue"), encapsulate Israel's obligations to their God and to each other. The first three (vv. 1–11) express Israel's exclusive relationship with Yahweh: they may not worship other deities or worship Yahweh incorrectly. The latter obligation means no images of any deity (including Yahweh), no improper use of Yahweh's name (which he has only recently revealed in 6:3), and remembrance of the Sabbath. The latter seven (vv. 12–17) concern relationships within Israelite society; they ensure protection of each Israelite's elders, life, marriage, property, and reputation.

Nowadays, the Decalogue is often memorialized in religious and secular settings as an example of universal law, but the commandments are as much a product of their ancient Israelite environment as the rest of the Bible. For example, the use of masculine singular verbs and pronouns indicates that the intended audience of the commandments was individual Israelite men, and slavery is mentioned as an acceptable part of society. These aspects remind us that Israelite culture is different from our own, and its laws must be translated to our context if they are to play a meaningful role in our lives and relationships. Remarkably, this kind of cultural translation takes place within the Bible itself. The Decalogue is repeated in Deuteronomy 5:6–21 with some variations. These changes are minor but nonetheless show that even in ancient Israel itself it was necessary to translate these commandments, and the covenantal relationship they represent, into new contexts.

Looking Ahead

So far, this chapter has focused on the divine covenants in the books of Genesis and Exodus, but these are not the only biblical books in which covenants play a significant role. As we will see in this concluding section, subsequent books take the concept into new directions. For example, when Jerusalem is destroyed in 586 BCE and the people of Judah are exiled to Babylon for forty-seven years, the prophet Jeremiah reformulates the Sinai covenant for this new reality. The same is true for Jesus of Nazareth, who in the first century CE announced the establishment of a new covenant in his blood. New circumstances in Israel's history call for new formulations of the divine covenant.

Before looking at these examples (and later in chapter 4, on kingship, we will study God's covenant with David), we should note that, like the three covenants examined above, these new expressions of God's covenantal relationship do not abrogate the older ones. Rather, just as the Noahide covenant provided a backdrop for God's more particular covenant with Abraham, which was later reinforced with the Sinai covenant, successive iterations of God's covenant build on their predecessors, sometimes explicitly so. Returning to the analogy of marriage, we might compare these subsequent covenants to the renewal of wedding vows. When a couple renews their vows, they may make changes to their original vows or add new ones that reflect new aspects of their marriage; such revision doesn't undermine the vows they made at their wedding but builds on them. Like all relationships, the couple's marriage has grown and changed, and they want this growth reflected in the formal expression of their commitment to each other.

This perspective helps us understand the way the prophet Jeremiah innovates God's covenant with Israel in the wake of the Babylonian Exile. The exile was a time of crisis and upheaval; the covenant seemed to be broken. According to the prophets, the people of Israel had failed to uphold their covenantal obligations—exclusive worship of Yahweh and just treatment of each other—and their iniquity compelled God to abandon his protection of them. This punishment is not the final word on covenants, however; although the prophets inveighed against Israel for its transgressions, they later express God's desire to renew the covenant. An inspiring statement of this desire comes from Jeremiah:

> The days are surely coming, says the LORD, when I will make a new covenant with the house of Israel and the house of Judah. It will not be like the covenant that I made with their ancestors when I took them by the hand to bring them out of the land of Egypt— a covenant that they broke, though I was their husband, says the LORD. But this is the covenant that I will make with the house of Israel after those days, says the LORD: I will put my law within them, and I will write it on their hearts; and I will be their God, and they shall be my people. *(31:31–33)*

This passage captures the divine desire to restore his relationship with Israel but also the recognition that changes must be made. At the heart of that relationship remains the promise "I will be your God, and you will be my people," but the exilic reality calls for a revision of the old agreement, which God had established at Sinai.

The most significant shift in this new covenant is that the law, which at Sinai had been written on stone tablets, will now be written on the hearts of individual Israelites. From now on each person is responsible for his or her own righteousness. This insistence on individual responsibility is meant to assure the exiled Jews that they will no longer be punished for the sins of the previous generation (Jer 31:29–30; Ezek 18:1–4), but it also reflects a new social reality in exile. Before the exile, Israelites had depended on kings and prophets to mediate and interpret God's covenant for them, but in exile, neither office could be counted on to bring the people back to the covenant. Given this reality, Jeremiah reimagines the covenant without the middlemen; from now on, it will be inscribed on the heart of each Israelite.

This change represents another example of God adjusting the covenant to meet the Israelites where they are. What worked in the Sinai covenant was no longer feasible in the exile, and God is willing and able to accommodate this new reality. God is still God, and the covenantal formula—I will be your God and you will be my people—endures, but it is clear to God and the prophets that certain features of the covenant must be revised, if it is to remain a viable expression of his loving relationship with Israel.

Jeremiah's innovative approach to the Sinai covenant provides crucial background for another renewal of God's covenant with Israel, namely, the new covenant established by Jesus. This covenant is an essential feature of the New Testament; in fact, the very phrase "New Testament" comes in part from the Latin word *testamentum*, which means "covenant." The use of this word as a title for the canon of Scripture written by the followers of Jesus indicates the centrality of this concept for Christianity. However, this new covenant does not nullify the Old Testament covenants that have preceded it, just as Jeremiah's "new covenant" did not erase its predecessors, nor did Abraham's covenant cancel the Noahide covenant. As this chapter has demonstrated, new expressions of God's covenantal relationship do not displace earlier ones but take them in a new direction according to new circumstances.

The new covenant of Jesus is announced at the Last Supper when Jesus takes the cup and declares, "This is my blood of the covenant, which is poured out for many" (Mark 14:24; see also Matt 26:28; Luke 22:20; 1 Cor 11:25). The phrase "blood of the covenant" refers back to the Sinai covenant, specifically Exodus 24:6–8. In these verses, Moses takes the blood of the animals sacrificed as part of the covenant ceremony and splashes it on the altar and on the people. This blood is a symbol of the covenant's ratification.

This background deepens our appreciation of Jesus' words at the Last Supper. First of all, by evoking the words that ratified the Sinai covenant, Jesus establishes continuity between it and the new covenant that he is instituting. Like all of the covenants we have examined in this chapter, Jesus' covenant must be viewed against the backdrop of earlier covenants. There are new elements of course; most notably, it is Jesus' own sacrificial blood, rather than the blood of animals, that ratifies the covenant, and the covenantal community will be a more expansive body than the community established by the Sinai covenant. Such innovations do not cancel preceding covenants but build on them by renewing the longstanding relationship between God and Israel for a new time and context.

This chapter's examination of covenants in the Bible has shown the importance of this concept for understanding God's love for creation in general and Israel in particular. Biblical covenants also remind us of our obligation to reciprocate that love with God and each other. As we saw with creation in the previous chapter, covenants cannot be examined in isolation, but each must be viewed as part of an ongoing relationship that transforms over time. This view is necessary not just for individual covenants but also for the entire Old Testament ("old covenant"), especially as it relates to the New Testament ("new covenant"). Although we regard "old" and "new" as antonyms, the preceding study of biblical covenants invites us to see the Old and New Testaments as standing in continuity rather than opposition. They are part of the same story and together constitute the Christian Bible. Moreover, the biblical depiction of covenants challenges our modern tendency to conflate "old" with "obsolete" and "new" with "better." As this chapter has shown, the "old" in Old Testament simply refers to an earlier stage in God's relationship with Israel, a stage that, far from being nullified by subsequent covenants, is indispensable for understanding later developments in this loving and life-giving relationship.

QUESTIONS *for* REFLECTION

Like the creation stories, biblical covenants have been adapted from Near Eastern models. What does this adaptation tell us about the biblical writers' engagement with the world around them and how they understood Israel's unique witness to the world?

What are the challenges and advantages of having multiple covenants in effect in Israel's relationship with their God? How can Christians today bring the rich history of covenants to bear on the new covenant established by Jesus?

How do biblical covenants express both God's care for all people and creation and God's unique relationship with Israel?

THREE

PROPHECY

Prophecy in the Old Testament begins with Moses. Although he is not the first in the Bible to be called a prophet (see Gen 20:7; Exod 7:1; 15:20), his career and leadership provide the model for many of the prophets that come after him. His primacy is made explicit in Deuteronomy 18 when God promises to "raise up for [Israel] a prophet like [Moses] from among their own people" (v. 18). Moses was unique in his direct access to God; he alone was able to converse with God "face-to-face" (Exod 33:11; 34:33–35; Num 12:8). Although no other prophet could equal his unique relationship with God (Deut 34:10), God promises that in each generation he will raise up a prophet like Moses.

In fact, the delegation of Moses's prophetic gifts and duties took place even before this promise from God. In Numbers 11, God relieved the burden of Moses's leadership by sharing his spirit with seventy elders who had gathered around the Tent of Meeting and fell into a one-time "prophetic frenzy" (vv. 16–17, 24–25). However, so great was God's generosity with the spirit that it spilled over to two men who had not joined the seventy but stayed in the camp; they too received Moses's prophetic spirit (v. 26). This generosity upset Joshua, who complained to Moses and received a rebuke in return: "Are you jealous for my sake? Would that all the Lord's people were prophets, and that the Lord would put his spirit on them!" (vv. 28–29). This episode foreshadows God's promise in Deuteronomy 18 by highlighting

Moses as the prophet *par excellence* but also his willingness to share the unique gift he has received from God.

This understanding of Moses as both unique interlocutor with God and prototypical prophet helps us identify the essential task of the biblical prophet. Moses was, above all, a mediator between God and the people of Israel, and the prophets who follow his example continue this service. Sometimes this mediation means representing the people before God, as when Moses and other prophets persuade God to forgive Israel's sins (Exod 32:11–14; Amos 7:1–6), but most often it means the prophet witnessing God to the people. The content of this prophetic witness varies according to circumstances. The prophet expresses divine outrage at social injustice and idolatry but also proclaims the promise of God's renewal in the midst of crisis. The rest of this chapter will look at the different facets of prophetic ministry in the Bible, and I will illustrate each facet with well-known prophetic figures and biblical texts. Besides illustrating certain key features, the following examples are meant to show how these familiar figures and texts relate to each other within the framework of biblical prophecy.

Before proceeding to these key features, however, a few more introductory remarks are in order. First of all, prophecy is not, first and foremost, about predicting the future. Rather, the principal role of biblical prophets is to proclaim God's view of their *present* situation. Often this divine judgment of the present has future implications (e.g., God sees his people suffering and promises imminent relief, or God sees his people's sins and warns of impending punishment), but such visions of the future cannot be divorced from the prophet's present audience who first heard them.

As an analogy, consider the famous "I Have a Dream" speech of Dr. Martin Luther King Jr., who is regarded by many as a modern-day prophet. The speech imagines a future of racial justice and harmony, but no one would say the speech was a vision of the future with no relevance to his present audience. On the contrary, King was using this hopeful future to critique the racism of his present; any interpretation of the speech must begin with King's own context. Of course, the speech went on to have an impact far beyond King's initial audience, as "I Have a Dream" has continued to inspire and challenge Americans in the decades since he delivered it. The speech has held different meanings for these subsequent hearers, and each meaning is an integral part of the overall significance of the speech. Nonetheless, the starting point for any study of "I Have a Dream" should be the Civil Rights movement, in general, and the 1963 March on Washington, in particular.

This analogy applies to our understanding of biblical prophecy in several ways. First, we must take into account the historical setting of prophetic texts. Prophets were not mechanical conduits of divine words intended only for readers long after the original speakers were gone. Rather, the prophets were embedded in particular communities with particular challenges, and these historical circumstances shaped the prophetic words they received from God and delivered to the people. Our study of their testimony must attend to these circumstances.

Second, however, we recognize that biblical prophecy has been meaningful beyond a prophet's immediate context. What makes "I Have a Dream" so powerful is its ability to speak to instances of racial injustice beyond the situation King himself was addressing. Likewise, the testimony of biblical prophets has continued to resonate with Jews and Christians in ways the prophets themselves never could have predicted. That is why we still read the prophets today; their words speak to the hopes and challenges of our times. This "surplus of meaning" is especially apparent in the New Testament, which features Jesus as the ultimate fulfillment of Old Testament prophecy. This view of biblical prophecy was valid for Jesus and his followers, and it remains valid for Christians today. The key is to make room for all valid interpretations of prophetic texts, including what they meant to their original audience, what they meant to later communities, like the early Christians, and what they mean to us today.

Another aspect of biblical prophecy worth noting at the outset of this chapter concerns the very term "prophet," which comes from Greek *prophētēs* and denotes "one who speaks for (God)." Certainly, this meaning is consistent with the above description of the prophet as one who represents God to the people (and vice versa), but the Hebrew word for prophet accents a different feature of biblical prophecy. The most common term for "prophet" in Hebrew is *nabi'*, which literally means "the one who is called." Unlike Greek *prophētēs*, which defines prophets by what they do, Hebrew *nabi'* highlights God's role in appointing prophets.

An appreciation of this Hebrew word sheds light on other facets of biblical prophecy. First, the meaning of *nabi'* helps us understand why so many prophetic texts include an account of the call from God, which inaugurated the prophet's ministry (Exod 3; 1 Sam 3; 1 Kgs 19:19–21; 22:19–23; Isa 6; Ezek 2—3; Jer 1:4–19; Amos 7:14–16). Insofar as these call narratives establish the prophets as "ones who have been called," they are an integral part of their career, and often the call itself foreshadows aspects of their ministry. For example, the burning bush in the call of Moses anticipates the fiery presence of God that will help Moses lead the people out of Egypt (Exod 3:3; cf. 13:21–22; 24:17); the emphasis on God's holiness in Isaiah's call marks it as a key theme in the book (Isa 6:3; cf. 29:23; 49:7; 57:15); Jeremiah's appointment

as a "prophet to the nations" previews his ministry to Jews who
have been deported to distant lands (Jer 1:5; cf. chs. 29—31); and
the mantle that Elijah throws over Elisha's shoulders will play an
important role in a later episode (1 Kgs 19:19; cf. 2 Kgs 2:13–14).
Moreover, whereas "prophet" focuses our attention on their
speaking role, Hebrew *nabi'* invites us to view prophets as
more than mouthpieces. Biblical prophecy entails much more
than speaking; often prophets act out the word of God in dramatic fashion. For example, the prophet Ahijah tore a garment
into twelve pieces to symbolize tearing of the kingdom from
Solomon (1 Kgs 11:30–31); and Jeremiah built a yoke as a symbol
of subjugation (Jer 27:2). Other times, the prophets' own lives
provide the medium for their message, and this embodiment
of prophetic witness demonstrates the personal cost of their
vocation. For example, Jeremiah foreshadows future decima-
tion by remaining unmarried and childless (Jer 16:1–4); Isaiah
and Ezekiel degrade themselves like prisoners of war to show
their audience the fate that awaits them (Isa 20; Ezek 4—5); and
Hosea gives his children names that represent God's rejection
of Israel (Hos 1:4–9). These examples show us that while speech
was essential to prophets' vocation, performance and embodiment were equally important modes of their witness. As we turn
now to the key features of biblical prophecy, we will see all three
modes employed by the prophets of ancient Israel.

Key Features of Biblical Prophecy

There is not enough space in this chapter to work through all
of the prophetic texts of the Old Testament. That task would
require an entire book! Instead I will highlight four key features and trace them through the prophetic books. These books
include the so-called Writing Prophets (i.e., books that represent

the written testimony of Isaiah, Jeremiah, Ezekiel, and the twelve minor prophets) as well as the books of Samuel and Kings, which contain many stories *about* prophets. (In fact, in Jewish tradition Samuel and Kings, along with Joshua and Judges, are called the "Former Prophets" for this reason, and in the Jewish Bible these books are followed by the "Latter Prophets," which are the same as the Writing Prophets.) These stories about prophets offer valuable information about their lives and ministry and fill out the picture drawn by the Writing Prophets' own words. Already I have named divine calling and mediation as defining features of biblical prophecy, and in the space that remains I will add four more facets, which are attested in both the Former and the Writing Prophets. The four are the communal setting of prophecy, its relationship to kingship, its advocacy for the poor, and its visions of restoration.

PROPHETS ARE MEMBERS OF COMMUNITIES

When we read passages from the Writing Prophets, we can sometimes imagine the prophet as an isolated individual, a religious iconoclast set apart from the rest of society. Within these books the voice of Isaiah (or Jeremiah, or Amos, etc.) stands out in forceful singularity, and we can overlook the communal context in which the prophets worked. For this reason, it is valuable to highlight biblical texts that depict prophets within their communities. Most of these prophetic communities were probably small groups, but we also get a few references to prophecy on a much larger scale. The story of the prophet Micaiah, for example, mentions that the king of Israel employed about four hundred (!) prophets to give him advice on various matters (1 Kgs 22:6; cf. 1 Kgs 18:19). That's an extraordinary number and probably not typical; only a king could afford to keep so many prophets on retainer. But despite its exceptionality, the number is helpful because it expands our perspective of the context within which prophets lived and worked.

An especially instructive example of the communal setting of prophecy comes from the careers of Elijah and his protégé Elisha. When it came time for God to take Elijah into heaven, he and Elisha visited prophetic communities of various towns (2 Kgs 2), the last of which consisted of fifty men (v. 7). These communities are called "the sons of the prophets," though modern translations often drop "sons" in favor of "company" or "disciples." This translation is understandable but misses a feature of the prophetic community, which becomes clear when Elijah ascends into heaven. As he departs, Elisha calls after him, "Father, father!" (v. 12). Taken together, the references to "sons" and "father" suggest that prophetic communities addressed each other with familial language, which may have included maternal designations. After all, women prophets are well-attested in the Old Testament (e.g., Miriam in Exodus 15:20, Isaiah's wife in Isaiah 8:3, Huldah in 2 Kings 22:13–14, and Noadiah in Nehemiah 6:14), and Deborah is called both a prophetess and a "mother in Israel" (Judg 4:4; 5:7).

These designations don't mean that the prophets couldn't have families of their own. Shortly after Elijah's ascension, we learn that at least one member of his community had a wife and children (2 Kgs 4:1). The key insight from 2 Kings 2 is that even a seeming loner like Elijah is part of a larger community of prophets who regard him as a father figure and continue his prophetic ministry after his departure. Indeed, after Elijah leaves, Elisha takes up his mantle and is recognized by the fifty as their new leader (v. 15). Moreover, the stories we have about Elijah only survive because the community around him saved them for posterity. If it were not so, if Elijah were a lone ranger with no colleagues or disciples, the record of his career would be lost. Although Elijah (and later Elisha) have the starring roles in these stories and their prophetic witness of justice and healing is what inspires us most, they, like all religious authorities, depend on their community of faith to recognize and support the leadership to which God has called them.

Another window into the communal character of biblical prophecy comes from 1 Samuel 10, which recounts Saul's anointing by the prophet Samuel. We will discuss the anointing itself in the next subsection, but what is interesting here is Saul's encounter with a band of prophets a few verses later. Samuel had predicted that Saul "will meet a band of prophets coming down from the shrine with harp, tambourine, flute, and lyre playing in front of them; they will be in a prophetic frenzy" (v. 5). Not only does Saul meet this band of prophets, "he fell into a prophetic frenzy along with them" (v. 10; cf. 1 Sam 19:20–24). This story reveals fascinating details about prophets in ancient Israel. First and most relevant to this subsection, some of them traveled together as a group, and their gift of prophecy could spread to others, as it did to Saul. His "prophetic frenzy" echoes the story in Numbers 11 of the two who stayed in the camp but still received the prophetic spirit. Both 1 Samuel 10 and Numbers 11 depict prophecy as a gift of the divine spirit that is received within prophetic communities but also shared outside that community.

Two other noteworthy details of this story are the prophets' musicality (cf. Exod 15:20), and their association with a shrine. The latter detail is especially significant because it provides a counterbalance to prophetic critiques of worship (e.g., Amos 5:21–24; Hos 6:6; Mic 6:6–8; Isa 1:12–16). Given the harshness of these critiques, we might suppose that the prophets rejected worship, but other texts reveal that many prophets were at home in sanctuaries and among priests (1 Sam 1:24—3:21; 9:11–15;

Isa 6:1; Jer 1:1; Ezek 1:3; 40—48). These texts show that, while prophets certainly denounced worship when it was divorced from righteous behavior and devotion to God, they did not reject it altogether. Rather their critique is a cry to reform the worship that was dear to them.

When we turn to the Writing Prophets, the evidence for prophetic communities is more oblique but still perceptible. As with the Elijah traditions discussed above, the best evidence may be the survival of the prophetic books themselves. If not for communities that supported, recorded, preserved, and curated the work of the Writing Prophets, their testimonies would have perished along with the prophets themselves. One reference to such community is found in Isaiah 8:16, in which the prophet gives the command to "bind up the testimony, seal the teaching among my disciples." In this verse the prophet acknowledges his disciples and the role that they will play in the continuation of his ministry. In fact, the rest of the Book of Isaiah represents the fulfillment of his command, since scholars regard chapters 40—66 as the work of unnamed disciples of Isaiah who applied his prophetic vision to new circumstances. Whereas Isaiah himself worked in Jerusalem in the eighth century BCE, chapters 40—55 are addressed to the Jews exiled in Babylon in the mid-sixth century BCE, and chapters 56—66 to Jews in the late–sixth century BCE who had returned to Jerusalem from Babylon. Each set of chapters represents a new development in the prophetic tradition of Isaiah and attests to the enduring power of his original vision and ministry. The communal context of prophecy helps us understand the networks that supported prophets and enabled their work to endure beyond their own careers.

Similar references can be found in the books of Jeremiah and Ezekiel. For example, there would be no Book of Jeremiah if not for his scribe Baruch, who wrote out the prophet's words. In one famous chapter (Jer 36), Baruch takes dictation from Jeremiah and delivers the scroll to the king of Judah who burns it as soon as he hears its contents. Afterward, God instructs Jeremiah who instructs Baruch to copy the original words and many more onto a new scroll. (This story has comforted me whenever I've lost a computer file!) Besides Baruch, Jeremiah mentions officials in Jerusalem who support his work. Especially noteworthy are members of the Shaphan family, whom he mentions by name (Jer 26:24; 29:3; 36:10–12; 39:14).

The evidence for Ezekiel's community of support is not as specific as these references but is similarly significant. Ezekiel was among the first wave of Jewish exiles to Babylon in 597 BCE, and his career takes place among these exiles (1:1). While much of his prophetic critique is directed at the Jews back in Jerusalem, Ezekiel's fellow exiles represent a support system for him. He sits among them for seven days in stunned silence after his initial vision of God (3:15), and they are the ones who listen to his account of a subsequent vision (11:25).

Taken together, these biblical references show that, although prophets were often unpopular and felt alienated from their societies, they were not isolated from all communal life. Rather, they were surrounded by communities, who recognized their prophetic authority, supported their work, and preserved their writings.

PROPHETS CHALLENGE ROYAL POWER

An essential feature of biblical prophets was the check they provided on the power of kings. Kingship will be the focus of the next chapter, and there we will highlight the positive contributions of kings and the importance of kingship to biblical theology. Here, however, we will look at kings through their encounters with prophets, which yield a less positive picture. Prophecy and kingship became institutions within ancient Israel at the same time, and the two offices remained linked throughout Israel's history. Their interactions were often tense, as prophets called out kings for their unjust treatment of people and their lack of faith in God. Prophets were the only ones with the status and authority to challenge kings in this way, as we will see in the examples that comprise this subsection.

Prophets view kingship with suspicion because they consider it a diminishment of God's kingship. When God finally consents to the people's demand for a king, he poignantly tells the prophet Samuel, "They have rejected me from being king over them" (1 Sam 8:7; cf. Judg 8:23). Indeed, the people request a king because they want to be "like other nations" (1 Sam 8:5, 20), but this desire contravenes the basic premise of the covenant between God and Israel. As we saw last chapter, the covenant established God as Israel's sovereign who ensures their safety and prosperity and expects their exclusive fidelity in return. This special relationship makes Israel "a treasured possession out of all the people…a priestly kingdom and a holy nation" (Exod 19:5–6). From the perspective of prophets like Samuel, Israel's desire to be "like other nations" surrenders part of their unique witness to God's holiness and justice.

Samuel was the strongest voice against kingship in Israel (1 Sam 8:10–18), but once it became inevitable, he showed the crucial role that prophets could play in keeping God's sovereignty front and center. God would allow Israel to have a king but would reserve the right to choose him, and this divine choice would be expressed through the prophet. As God's representative among the Israelites, the prophet is tasked with anointing the one God has selected (and will empower) to be king. This ritual of anointing is performed on Israel's first kings, Saul (1 Sam 10:1) and David (1 Sam 16:13), and by other prophets on subsequent kings (e.g., 1 Kgs 1:45; 2 Kgs 9:3). It marks the beginning of a king's reign but also signifies the king's dependency on prophets and the divine authority they represent. The prophet's role as God's agent is clear when Samuel anoints Saul but makes God, rather than himself, the subject of the action: "The Lord has anointed you ruler over his people Israel" (1 Sam 10:1).

Prophets were instrumental not only in authorizing kings to rule in Israel but in stripping them of their royal power. When Israel's first king, Saul, disobeys God and God regrets having made him king (1 Sam 15:11; 15:35), Samuel is the one who announces the demise of his kingship (1 Sam 15:22–29). Likewise, it is the prophet Ahijah who declares to Jeroboam that God has decided to tear ten tribes from Solomon's kingdom and give them to Jeroboam (1 Kgs 11:29–32). In both cases the annulment of kingship is accompanied by the same prophetic action; a ripped garment is held up by Samuel and Ahijah as a symbol of the power torn from the kings. Other examples of this prophetic role occur throughout the prophetic books, e.g., Elijah declares the end of the Omride dynasty (1 Kgs 21:20–22), Amos the end of Jeroboam II (Amos 7:9), and Jeremiah the end of Jehoiachin (Jer 22:24–30). Thus the divine authority embodied by prophets was expressed as much in their rejection of kings as in their establishment of their rule.

These rejections are extreme cases, but they are related to a task that is central to the work of biblical prophets, namely, their habit of challenging kings to rule with the justice and righteousness God expects of them, and when kings fail to live up to these expectations, the prophets call out their iniquity and declare consequences. Examples of prophetic challenges to royal abuse of power abound in the Bible, but a few famous episodes are worth mentioning. When king David impregnates Bathsheba and orchestrates the death of her husband, the prophet Nathan rebukes him for his transgressions and announces his punishment (2 Sam 11—12); when king Ahab and queen Jezebel arrange for Naboth to be killed so that they can seize his vineyard, the prophet Elijah condemns their wickedness (1 Kgs 21); and when king Ahaz doubts that God will deliver Judah from its enemies, the prophet Isaiah chides him and offers the child Immanuel as a sign of God's fidelity to his people (Isa 7). These examples show the unique ability of prophets to stand up to the highest authority in the kingdom. Because they represent an even higher authority, prophets are empowered to challenge kings when necessary.

PROPHETS CHAMPION THE POOR

The examples of Bathsheba (and her husband) and Naboth touch on another fundamental feature of biblical prophecy, which is attested throughout Scripture, namely, prophets' advocacy for the poor and marginalized. They stand up for those who cannot stand up for themselves. This advocacy is especially apparent in the prophets' concern for widows, orphans, and aliens, who lack the support of a kinship system and therefore represent the most vulnerable members of Israelite society. For the prophets they represent a benchmark of justice within the larger society. If the well-being of widows, orphans, and aliens is protected, then the overall health of Israel is good, but if they are not protected, their hardship is a sign of deeper and more pervasive injustice in society.

The prevalence of this trio throughout the prophetic books is remarkable. Prophets from every period of biblical history demand that the people and leaders of Israel remember the widow, the orphan, and the alien (Isa 1:17, 23; 9:17; 10:2; Jer 5:28; 7:6; 22:3; Ezek 22:7; Zec 7:10; Mal 3:5). Besides exhorting Israelites to care for these most vulnerable, prophets practice what they preach by tending to their needs. The prophet Elijah, for example, ministers to a widow in Zarephath who is on the verge of starvation; he miraculously multiplies her flour and oil, and later he revives her son after he falls ill and appears lifeless (1 Kgs 17:8–24). Elijah's protégé Elisha performs a similar miracle for a widow whose creditor threatens debt slavery for her children (2 Kgs 4:1–7).

Prophets' special concern for widows, orphans, and aliens is not the only way they express commitment to justice. Throughout the prophetic books we find verses in which they decry other forms of injustice. Amos is outraged at food vendors who rig the scales so that they can overcharge their customers (8:4–6) and at the rich who revel in luxury and are oblivious to the ruin all around them (6:4–6); Isaiah addresses judicial wrongs by indicting those who use the legal system to oppress the poor (10:1–2); Micah exposes exploitative real estate practices that rob families of their legacies (2:1–2); Zephaniah rails against the leaders of Jerusalem for setting an example of corruption that undermines justice (3:1–7); and Hosea shows how idolatry obstructs not only justice and righteousness but also steadfast love and mercy (2:16–20). All of these examples are applications of the prophets' commitment to justice and right relationship with God and within the covenantal community.

As a last word on justice, I want to emphasize the literary quality of the prophets. What makes them special is not just their advocacy for the poor; indeed, we can find similar advocacy in the legal texts, which likewise ensure protection for widows, orphans, and aliens (e.g., Exod 22:20–22; Deut 10:17–19; 24:17–22), and in wisdom literature, which includes the care for the poor (Prov 14:21; 22:22; 31:9, 20). But neither genre matches the forcefulness of the prophets' poetry. Amos, for example, doesn't just call for right action but insists that "justice roll down like waters, and righteousness like an ever-flowing stream" (5:24), and Isaiah doesn't just accuse leaders of oppressing the poor but of "crushing my people [and] grinding the face of the poor" (3:15). The Book of Isaiah also gives us memorable images, such as "oaks of righteousness" (61:3) and "the yoke of injustice" (58:6, 9), and who could forget Micah's famous command "to do justice, and to love kindness (Heb. *ḥesed*), and to walk humbly with God" (6:8)? Many other examples could be cited, but these will suffice to show that the biblical prophets are valuable not only for what they say and *how* they say it. To their audience, including us today, they give language and imagery that inspire action on behalf of the poor and vulnerable.

PROPHETS OFFER HOPE FOR RESTORATION

Nowadays, when communities of faith use the adjective "prophetic," they most often have in mind the prophets' tendency to challenge power and insist on social justice. As we have seen above, these features are essential to the ministry of biblical prophets, but prophets were also committed to consolation and forgiveness. Biblical prophecy is contextual; when circumstances call for judgment and critique, the prophets are fierce in their expression of God's anger at injustice, and they set forth punishment for the people that is commensurate with their sin. But in times of catastrophe, be it the punishment they had declared or some other calamity, the prophets offer visions of renewal that inspire hope in God's people. Thus, to be "prophetic" also means consoling people in the midst of crisis and giving them hope in God's ability to restore the broken parts of our lives and world. These visions of restoration most often occur in the work of the exilic prophets. Ministering to the Jews who had been deported to Babylon, these prophets insisted that God had not forgotten or abandoned his people but would soon renew them and bring them back to Jerusalem. This prophetic mission is captured beautifully in Isaiah 40—55. These chapters are the work of an anonymous prophet who continued the ministry of Isaiah to an exilic audience. The famous opening lines of chapter 40 announce the end of Jerusalem's punishment and the beginning of her restoration:

> Comfort, O comfort, my people, says your God.
> Speak tenderly to Jerusalem and cry to her
> that she has served her term,
> that her penalty is paid...
> In the wilderness prepare the way of the LORD
> make straight in the desert a highway for our God...
> He will feed his flock like a shepherd;
> he will gather the lambs in his arms,
> and carry them in his bosom
> and gently lead the mother sheep. *(vv. 1, 3, 11)*

These comforting words are good news for the exiled Jews who felt forsaken by God (Isa 40:27; 49:14). The prophet insists that God has not forgotten them but is coming to be with them and will bring them back to Jerusalem. The imagery of highway and shepherd evokes the Exodus and holds forth the promise of a new Exodus by which God will reconstitute his people in Zion (see also 41:17–20; 42:16; 43:16–21). Elsewhere in Isaiah 40–55 the prophet emphasizes God's creative power, both on a cosmic scale (40:12–14, 21–31; 43:1; 44:24–28) and on more mundane levels. For example, God is compared to a woman in childbirth (42:14) and a nursing mother (49:15), and his divine word is likened to rain that brings forth fresh sprouts (55:10–11). All of these images highlight God's power and desire to restore his people, and this promise of restoration is just as central to biblical prophecy as social critique. The prophet's essential task is to express God's will to his people, and when the people need divine consolation in times of crisis, the prophet is there to provide it.

Moreover, the poetic virtuosity we observed in the prophets' call for justice is also apparent in their visions of restoration. The above citations from Isaiah 40—55 are good examples of this artistry, and many more could be cited from the prophetic books. Elsewhere in the Book of Isaiah, for example, we find hope for a future so peaceful that wolf and lamb, leopard and kid, calf and lion will live together in harmony in Zion (11:6–8) and also the vision of Zion shining forth as a beacon of light to all peoples (2:2–5; 60:1–22). Through Jeremiah, God promises to renew his covenant with his people by giving them a new heart (Jer 24:7; 31:33; cf. Ezek 36:26–27), and Ezekiel envisions God reviving the dry bones of his people and leading them back to Zion (Ezek 37:1–14).

These are some of the more famous visions of restoration we find in the prophets, and they show that biblical prophecy is more than a critique of injustice; it is also a commitment to the renewal of God's people. Both are essential ingredients in the work of prophets, and both depend on the ability of the prophets to understand their context and to offer God's perspective on it. This ability to read "signs of the times" must be included in our understanding of the prophets as inspired figures. Most often we associate their inspiration with their unique relationship with God and with their extraordinary imagination, and these aspects of their ministry certainly attest to their privileged insight. But just as inspired is their discernment of their own circumstances and their ability to offer the words that the people of God need to hear.

Looking Ahead: Prophecy in the New Testament

That prophecy plays an important role in the New Testament is obvious simply from the explicit references to Jesus as a prophet. For example, Jesus' remark after his rejection in Nazareth that "prophets are not without honor, except in their own hometown" (Mark 6:4; Matt 13:57; Luke 4:24) implies that he regarded himself as a prophet. Furthermore, when Jesus asks, "Who do people say that I am?" his disciples' answer indicates that many shared this view of his ministry (Mark 8:27–28; Matt 16:13–14; Luke 9:18–19). The significance of prophecy for New Testament authors is also apparent from the many quotations taken from the prophets. Of the almost three hundred quotations from the Old Testament in the New Testament, approximately a third come from the prophetic books. Some of these quotations, such as Isaiah 40:3, 56:7, 60:1–2, and Daniel 7:13, are cornerstones of the gospel narratives. Thus, the prophetic books of the Old Testament, besides offering in their own right a powerful witness of divine justice and compassion, provide crucial background for understanding Jesus' ministry and the writings of his followers, who interpreted his career as the work of a prophet.

The identification of Jesus as a prophet takes on even more significance when we situate his prophetic activity in the context of first-century CE Judaism. According to Jewish tradition, prophecy ceased at the time of the fifth-century BCE priest Ezra, who helped rebuild the community of Jews who had returned from the Babylonian Exile. Although scholars debate the extent of this cessation, in general they agree that traditional prophecy stopped serving as a mode of divine revelation. So between the fifth century BCE and the first century CE there was no new prophetic revelation. There was, however, the expectation that prophecy would be restored in the future, and this fulfillment of this hope would be a sign of the Messiah and the final redemption of Israel. Thus, the depiction of Jesus as a prophet indicates not just the Old Testament inspiration of his ministry but also its significance in the larger divine plan.

Knowing the importance of the Old Testament prophecy for understanding Jesus' ministry, we will use the last part of this chapter to push the comparison further and show how Jesus continued in his work the four characteristics of biblical prophecy described above.

First, the prophetic ministry of Jesus took place within a communal context. We all know that Jesus was surrounded by disciples and that he was especially close to the twelve apostles, but against the backdrop of Old Testament prophecy we can see parallels between Jesus' relationship with his apostles and prophets with their disciples. For example, Jesus' call of the first disciples seems to be modeled on Elijah's call of Elisha (1 Kgs 19:19–21). In both cases, the disciples are depicted in the midst of their daily occupations when they are called by a prophetic figure. The first apostles follow Jesus, just as Elisha followed Elijah.

Moreover, after Jesus returned to the Father in heaven, his apostles continued his earthly ministry, just as the work of Old Testament prophets, like Elijah and Isaiah, was continued by their disciples. This dynamic is most apparent in Luke-Acts, which features the apostles in Acts performing Jesus' ministry of healing and preaching, as described in Luke. They are able to continue this work because they have been empowered by the Holy Spirit (Acts 1:8), just as Old Testament prophets shared their prophetic spirit with disciples who would succeed them. Thus, a deeper understanding of Old Testament prophecy enriches our view of Jesus' relationship with his disciples and the legacy of his ministry among them.

Second, Jesus challenged those in power. It is clear from the gospel narratives that Jesus encountered considerable opposition from the political and religious authorities. The kingdom of God he preached posed a threat to these authorities because it asserted God's dominion over temporal rulers. This focus on divine authority over against earthly authority recalls the ways that Old Testament prophets checked the power of the king in the name of God's justice and righteousness. The incident in the gospels that most captures this prophetic inheritance is Jesus' action in the temple, when he expelled the sellers and buyers and disrupted the money changers (Mark 11:15–19; Matt 21:12–13; Luke 19:45–48; John 2:13–17). This action was a direct challenge to the temple leaders, who held power in Jerusalem and allowed, if not supported, the commercial activity that Jesus condemns. The prophetic character of his temple action is especially revealed in the quotation of Isaiah 56:7, which calls for the temple to be "a house of prayer for all peoples." In this episode Jesus continues the prophetic tradition of challenging political and religious authorities, and as with the Old Testament prophets, his challenge to power endangered his own life.

Third, Jesus was committed to the most vulnerable members of his society. Evidence that this commitment was essential

to his mission comes at the beginning of Jesus' public ministry in Luke. This chapter describes his visit to the synagogue
in Nazareth, where he read aloud a passage from the Book of
Isaiah:

> The Spirit of the Lord is upon me,
>> because he has anointed me
>>> to bring good news to the poor.
> He has sent me to proclaim release to the captives
>> and recovery of sight to the blind,
>>> to let the oppressed go free,
> to proclaim the year of the Lord's favor.
> *(Luke 4:18–19; cf. Isa 60:1–2; 58:6)*

After having read this passage, Jesus dramatically declares that
"today this scripture has been fulfilled in your hearing." Many
examples from the gospels could be cited to demonstrate Jesus'
preferential option for the poor, but this passage in particular
highlights the prophetic roots of his concern for, and care of, the
poor and oppressed.

Finally, like many Old Testament prophets, Jesus offered hopeful visions of restoration. This hope for the future is expressed in
his teaching on the kingdom of God, which he often describes
with images of abundance, e.g., a seed that brings forth a hun-
dredfold yield (Mark 4:8) or a mustard seed that grows into an
enormous bush (Mark 4:30–32). Not all of Jesus' teaching on
the kingdom of God is rooted in Old Testament prophecy, but
one with clear antecedents in the prophetic books is the motif
of the banquet. The importance of feasting in Jesus' ministry is
clear from the multiple accounts of the feeding of the multi-
tudes. This miracle of abundance, which occurs in one form or

another six times in the gospels, seems to be modeled on a similar miracle in Elisha's career, when he multiplies twenty loaves to feed a hundred people and has some left over (2 Kgs 4:42–44).

The imagery of the banquet is also prominent in Jesus' parables on the kingdom of God. The parable of the great dinner, for example, compares the kingdom to a wedding banquet at which all are welcome (Matt 22:1–10). The banquet in this parable echoes a verse in the Book of Isaiah, which likewise uses a banquet to offer a vision of future abundance for all peoples: "On this mountain the LORD of hosts will make for all peoples a feast of rich food, a feast of well-aged wines, of rich food filled with marrow, of well-aged wines strained clear" (25:6). Thus, the image of the banquet, drawn from the Old Testament prophets, plays a role both in Jesus' ministry and his vision of the future. As a metaphor for the kingdom of God, the banquet reveals the present and future reality of God's reign.

QUESTIONS *for* REFLECTION

Who are some prophets in today's world and church, and how do they compare with the biblical portrayal of prophets?

Thinking about prophecy as not just speech but an embodied activity, what are some prophetic actions you have observed (or performed yourself)?

Thinking about the Hebrew term *nabi'*, how have you been "called" by God to play a prophetic role in your community of faith?

FOUR

KINGSHIP

LAST CHAPTER, WE LOOKED AT PROPHECY IN THE OLD TESTAMENT, AND WE NOTED THAT ONE OF ITS KEY DUTIES WAS TO PROVIDE A CHECK ON THE AUTHORITY OF KINGS. Prophets are suspicious of royal power, and if the prophetic books were the only evidence we had for kingship in the Bible, we would share this negative perspective, which is first expressed in the Book of Deuteronomy. In chapter 17, just before the promise of a "prophet like Moses" in every generation, Moses foreshadows Israel's desire for a king and recommends a model of kingship with very limited power. According to Moses, the ideal king is one who defers to the law:

> When he has taken the throne of his kingdom, he shall have a copy of this law written for him…and he shall read in it all the days of his life…diligently observing all the words of this law and these statutes, neither exalting himself above other members of the community nor turning aside from the commandment. *(vv. 18–20).*
>
> *("Copy of the law" is Greek **deuteronomion**, which is where the book gets its name in the Christian canon.)*

Moses's advice presumes, and attempts to forestall, the tendency of kings to exalt themselves, and his view is typical of prophets in the Old Testament.

68

This dim view of kingship, however, is not the only biblical perspective on kingship. There is a countervailing perspective in the Old Testament that celebrates the king as nothing less than God's adopted son. When God establishes a covenant with David, he declares, "I will be a father to him, and he shall be a son to me" (2 Sam 7:14; see also Ps 89:26–27). According to this view, the king of Israel is the anointed one who establishes God's justice and righteousness throughout the land and delivers Israel from its enemies; he is God's covenantal partner who brings his steadfast love to the people.

Remarkably, these opposing views of kingship remain in tension throughout the Old Testament. In this way the biblical narrative mirrors the relationship between kingship and prophecy in ancient Israel. On the one hand, the two offices are interdependent. They arose at the same time in Israel's history and also came to an end around the same time after the Babylonian Exile. Throughout their parallel histories, kings depended on prophets to authorize their rule and give them advice, and many prophets depended on the king insofar as he employed them in the royal court. At times, their relationship could be strained; prophets challenged royal abuse of power, as we saw last chapter, and for their part, kings could pressure prophets and make their life difficult (cf. 1 Kgs 22). This complex relationship results in a variety of biblical perspectives on kingship, which reflect the mixed views held by the biblical writers themselves.

At the heart of these opposing views is a fundamental question: Is it possible for Israel to have a human king without diminishing the divine kingship of God? This question is not unlike the conundrum that is addressed in the first books of the Bible. There God faced the challenge of being in relationship with humanity in a way that preserved God's transcendence and

humans' free will. That process began with a number of false
starts and divine frustration before the Abrahamic and Sinai
covenants provided a successful framework for the divine-human relationship. A similar process of trial and error unfolds
with kingship in Israel; after several failed attempts at kingship,
God finds in David a human agent "after his own heart" (1 Sam
13:14). Ultimately, it is again a covenant, this time between God
and David, which strikes the balance between divine transcendence (God's kingship) and human agency (an earthly king).

This chapter will trace that process through the books of
Samuel and Kings, and along the way we will explore key languages and images associated with kingship, especially the term
messiah, i.e., the "anointed one." We will then look at what hap-
pens to kingship during the exilic and postexilic periods, when
the office loses its power and then disappears from the political
life of Judah but persists as a concept and symbol of future hope.
Finally, we will explore how the New Testament writers depict
Jesus as the fulfillment of that Davidic hope.

The Bumpy Road to Kingship

Although kingship will eventually be seen as a practical neces-
sity and a gift from God, its success was by no means certain. By
reviewing the tortuous and sometimes bumpy road to kingship,
we can see how the institution was shaped by Israel's needs as a
people and God's willingness to meet those needs. The beginnings of monarchy are found in the failure of the system of
judges that first governed the twelve tribes of Israel after their
settlement in the Promised Land. In theory, the tribes were
united by a shared lineage and history. They were descended
from the twelve sons of Jacob/Israel, who came with their father
to Egypt to escape the famine in Canaan (Gen 47—50). The

family of each brother grew into its own tribe, but the twelve were united by their common ancestor Jacob/Israel. Moreover, God's rescue of Israel from slavery in Egypt was an experience shared by all the tribes. The unifying effect of this event is clear from the covenant renewal ceremony at Shechem at the end of the Book of Joshua, where the tribes commemorate the Exodus as their shared history with God (Josh 24).

Their covenant is meant to bind them to God and also to each other, but in the Book of Judges that unity is tested and found wanting. According to the judge system, each tribe has its own leader, and when necessary, the tribes should combine their resources toward a common goal, such as defeating a common enemy in battle. But such cooperation is lacking in Deborah's battle against the Canaanites, and her victory song commemorates the tribes that came to her aid and those who did not (Judg 5:14–18). As the Book of Judges proceeds, the disunity of the tribes worsens. Eventually, they are not just failing to cooperate but actually fighting against each other. In Judges 12 we find the Gileadites at arms with the Ephraimites, and the book ends with a horrific story of the rape of the Levite's concubine, which leads to warfare between the tribe of Benjamin and the rest of the Israelites (chs. 19–21).

Overall the Book of Judges describes the steady devolution of the judge system and, in doing so, makes a case for centralized authority that is able to ensure cooperation among the tribes or, at the very least, to keep them from fighting against each other. The argument is made explicit in an editorial comment that is repeated four times at the end of the book: "In those days there was no king in Israel; (all the people did what was right in their own eyes)" (17:6; 18:1; 19:1; 21:25). The last two instances frame the story of the Levite's concubine and the ensuing warfare and thus express the editor's view of the root cause of this mayhem and its solution. According to this refrain and the overall narrative of Judges, a king is a necessary next step in the governance of the tribes of Israel.

Thus, the Book of Judges seems to be a strong endorsement of kingship, except that we find in the same book compelling arguments against kingship! Indeed, the two attempts in Judges to install a king demonstrate a clear downside to the office. The first comes at the end of Gideon's judgeship. He was so successful at defeating the Midianites, the Israelites make this request of him: "Rule over us, you and your son and your grandson also; for you have delivered us out of the hand of Midian" (Judg 8:22). Although they don't use the word "king," that is clearly what the Israelites have in mind. They want the stability of dynastic succession instead of the intermittent leadership of charismatic judges, whose gift of God's spirit does not pass to a successor. Even more telling is Gideon's rejection of their offer: "I will not rule over you, and my son will not rule over you; the LORD will rule over you" (8:23). In this response Gideon points to the conundrum at the heart of the biblical discourse on kingship, namely, how can Israel have a king without diminishing the divine kingship of God? Gideon doesn't think it's possible, and many of the biblical prophets would agree with him.

Soon after Gideon's refusal, we meet his son Abimelech, who is far less reluctant to rule as king, and the story of his rise and fall offers a warning to Israelites who might underestimate the desire for power that drives kings and sometimes results in bloodshed and destruction. Abimelech, whose name ironically means "my father is king," goes to Shechem, the very site of the tribes' covenant ceremony in Joshua 24, and offers himself as sole ruler instead of rule diffused among seventy leaders (Judg

9:2). When the lords of Shechem agree to his offer, he kills his seventy brothers and is installed as king (9:6).

Before long, the loyalties of the Shechemites shift to a new-comer, but Abimelech thwarts the usurpation by attacking the newcomer and the Shechemites, the same people who had made him king in the first place. He slaughters his own people; he destroys Shechem; and in a final sacrilegious atrocity, he sets fire to the temple in which men and women had taken refuge (9:42–49). This grim portrait of kingship contains a warning for Israel; those who gain such power will cling to it at all costs, even if it means destroying their own people. Remarkably, the narrator concludes the story of Abimelech by noting the people's culpability in the disaster: "God also made all the wickedness of the people of Shechem fall back on their heads" (9:57). Although Abimelech bears most of the guilt, the people are complicit because they consented to Abimelech's bid for exclusive power. Thus, the views on kingship in the Book of Judges are mixed. On the one hand, it is presented as the remedy for the divisions that have destabilized Israel, but on the other hand, the first examples of kingship in the narrative highlight the problems that come with it.

This ambivalence continues into the Book of Samuel where the issue of kingship takes center stage. The book opens on a hopeful note through the character of Hannah. At first, her personal struggles with barrenness seem to have nothing to do with kingship, but in the hymn she sings after God answers her prayer, she draws an analogy between herself and the future king (1 Sam 2). Her hymn begins and ends with the same language of praise, but the first verse refers to Hannah herself and the last verse to the king:

> "My heart exults in the Lord; my strength ("horn") is exalted in my God." *(v. 1)*

"He will give strength to his king, and exalt the power
("horn") of his anointed." *(v. 10)*

In between these two verses Hannah praises God's justice, which
humbles the arrogant and exalts the lowly. In this way, she shows
that a king of Israel is not incompatible with divine kingship
but an extension of God's rule. The king is the one whom God
will empower to vindicate the needy, just as God has supported
Hannah in her time of need. By correlating her own story of
redemption to the advent of kingship in Israel, Hannah foreshadows the positive ways that the king will carry out God's
will in Israel.

Hannah's son, Samuel, however, has a quite different perspective. As the last great leader of Israel before the monarchy,
Samuel served multiple roles in Israel; he is a prophet (1 Sam
3:20), a judge (1 Sam 7:6), and even a priest, based on his appren-
ticeship under the priest Eli (1 Sam 2:11; 3:1), his priestly vest-
ments (1 Sam 2:18), and his later role in presiding over sacrifices
(1 Sam 7:9–10; 10:8). Samuel is the one whom the Israelites
approach with their demand for a king: "Appoint for us, then,
a king to govern us, like other nations" (1 Sam 8:5). Right away,
we can note a problem with their request. They say that kingship
will make them "like other nations," but the whole point of the
Sinai covenant is for Israel to *not* be like the other nations. Their
election for a special relationship with God obliges them to be
"a priestly kingdom and a holy (literally, "set apart") nation"
(Exod 19:6). Again we confront the central conundrum of kingship, albeit from a different angle: Can Israel serve a human king
and still be the people uniquely called to serve God through
exclusive covenantal *ḥesed*? Hannah's hymn implies that the two
are compatible, but Samuel is less sanguine.

At this early stage of kingship, God shares Samuel's view. When the prophet reports the request to him, God poignantly replies, "Listen to the voice of the people in all that they say to you; for they have not rejected you, but they have rejected me from being king over them" (1 Sam 8:7). As a last resort, God instructs Samuel to tell the people "the ways of the king," and Samuel does so in a long speech (1 Sam 8:9–18). In it he describes everything the king will take from the people, namely, their children, fields, vineyards, orchards, slaves, and livestock, but the people are undeterred. "No!" they say. "But we are determined to have a king over us" (1 Sam 8:19). Finally, God relents, telling Samuel, "Listen to their voice and set a king over them" (1 Sam 8:22), and the next chapter narrates God's selection of Saul as the first king of Israel. He is the beginning of kingship in the Bible, but as this section has shown, the path to his appointment as king was hardly smooth or straight. Because kingship is ultimately remembered as a positive development in the history of Israel, especially when we think of king David, it is easy to overlook the lively debate that precedes its establishment. In fact, the debate continues even after the first kings have been anointed.

Messiah as a Title and Concept in the Bible

Before proceeding to these first kings of Israel, however, it will be worthwhile to discuss a key word related to kingship, namely, messiah (Heb. *mašîaḥ*), which means "anointed one." As a word and a concept, messiah will later take on great theological significance, but its origins are more mundane. In its initial use, "messiah" simply referred to the present king of Israel. He was the "anointed one" because anointing was the ritual act that marked the beginning of a king's reign. Thus Saul is the messiah; then David is the messiah; then Solomon is the messiah; and so on. In these early uses of the term, it does not connote future hope but instead designates the current king, regardless of his quality. Israel had its good kings, its mediocre kings, and its bad kings, and all of them were messiahs by virtue of the anointing that inaugurated their reigns.

How did the term develop from this mundane meaning to a title for the future king who would come at the end of time to deliver Israel from its enemies and set right once and for all the wrongs it had suffered? That process began with the hope that a new messiah in the near future would do a better job than the present messiah. For example, the king Ahaz (732–716 BCE) is criticized by the prophet Isaiah for pursuing questionable alliances during a military crisis rather than trusting God to deliver him from the threat (Isa 7). Shortly after this episode is the famous passage in Isaiah, declaring that

> The people who walked in darkness
>   have seen a great light;
> those who lived in a land of deep darkness—
>   on them light has shined…
> For a child has been born for us,
>   a son given to us;
> authority rests upon his shoulders;
>   and he is named
> Wonderful Counselor, Mighty God,
>   Everlasting Father, Prince of Peace.
> His authority shall grow continually,
>   and there shall be endless peace
> for the throne of David and his kingdom.
>   He will establish and uphold it
> with justice and with righteousness
>   from this time onward and forevermore. *(Isa 9:2, 6–7)*

It's difficult for Christians to hear this passage and not think of Jesus, but in the context of the Book of Isaiah, this passage expresses hope for a king in the near future who will succeed where Ahaz has failed. That king is Ahaz's son and successor Hezekiah, who is indeed remembered as a model of trust (2 Kgs 18—20, esp. 18:5; Isa 36—39). So this passage is "messianic" in the sense that it looks forward to a king who will more effectively carry out the duties of the office, but that hope was imminent rather than distant.

As Israel's history continues to unfold, the prospect of a near-future messiah who will set things right diminishes. As we shall see below, kingship shrinks during the exile and soon after disappears as a political reality in Judah. Messiahs no longer rule over the people of God. However, the concept of messiah persists and even grows in the Jewish imagination, but now this messianic hope was projected into the distant future. By the time of Jesus's life and ministry, there was a widespread expectation among Jews that the end times were imminent and would feature the advent of a messiah who would vindicate Israel once and for all. This view of messiah is the one we find in the New Testament (though, as we will see, Jesus puts his own spin on this view). It has come a long way from the word's original meaning in the books of Samuel and Kings, where it is simply another way to refer to the present king.

The Rise and Fall of Saul
The first of these messiahs to be anointed the king of Israel is Saul. As soon as the Israelites reject Samuel's warnings about "the ways of the king" and God concedes to their demand for a monarch (1 Sam 8), God reveals to Samuel that he has selected Saul as Israel's first anointed (9:16). When Samuel performs

the anointing, he declares to Saul, "The Lord has anointed (*mašaḥ*) you ruler over his people Israel" (10:1). The subject of the verb in this declaration is important; although Samuel has performed the ritual, he identifies God as the source of its efficacy. The anointing is a sign of divine approval and empowerment and represents the king's God-given authority to rule over Israel. This is the compromise that begins to resolve the tension between human and divine kingship. God will allow for a king to rule over the people but reserves the prerogative to select the officeholder. The Israelite king will not diminish divine kingship because God will choose righteous servants for the job, and this choice will be conveyed through prophets, who speak and act on God's behalf.

But even after this compromise, misgivings about kingship persist and surface early in Saul's reign. After Saul's private anointing by Samuel, there are two stories of his public acclamation as king. In the first, Saul is hiding behind baggage at the moment he is to be introduced as king (10:22)—hardly, a debut that inspires confidence! Indeed, the story concludes with a note that "some worthless fellows said, 'How can this man save us?' They despised him and brought him no present" (10:27). In the second story, Saul is acclaimed king after he leads Israel's army to victory, but the memory of those naysayers lingers. Some want to kill the doubters, but Saul prevents bloodshed and is renewed as king before all the people (11:12–14). He is king and God's anointed, but not everyone recognizes him as such.

These misgivings turn out to be well-founded, because Saul twice disobeys divine orders given by Samuel (1 Sam 13:7–15 [cf. 10:8]; 15:1–35). After the second disobedience, God makes a startling statement to Samuel: "I regret that I made Saul king, for he has turned back from following me, and has not carried out my commandments" (15:11). The verb for "regret" is the same one used of God's regret over the creation of humankind (Gen 6:6). The repetition highlights parallels between the two storylines. In both cases the free will that God has graciously given his people becomes a source of divine frustration. God's regret is not a sign of weakness but the cost of his willingness to make humankind in general and the king in particular true partners in the divine plan rather than automata of his will. God has selected Saul and anointed him king, but that doesn't guarantee that Saul will prove worthy of his appointment any more than the creation of humankind in God's image guarantees that they will imitate his care for creation and each other. In both cases, it takes time and some trial-and-error before God finds a lasting way to be in relationship with his people and their king. Saul's kingship, like Abimelech's, was a false start, and he is stripped of his rule. But the moment of his rejection contains the seed of a new hope, as Samuel foreshadows Saul's yet unnamed successor as "a man after [God's] own heart" (13:14).

David the Model Messiah

That man, we soon learn, is David, the youngest son of Jesse, and his kingship solves the conundrum of divine and human kingship. This success results from the affinity of David's heart for God and also from God's promise of forbearance when David and his successors make mistakes. Having learned from Saul's disobedience, God makes a covenant with David and his descendants that makes room for their imperfection. We will look at that covenant shortly; here we simply note that this covenant is the culmination of a process that began in the Book of Judges. The solution to reconciling divine and human kingship is God's role in selecting the king of Israel and God's merciful willingness to tolerate their mistakes, which are inevitable, as we know from Saul and will soon learn from David and Solomon. David is introduced in the chapter immediately after Saul's final rejection. God told Samuel to look for the new messiah among the sons of Jesse, but God rejects all the sons present. Only the youngest son who is out keeping the sheep remains, and when he arrives, God tells Samuel: "Rise and anoint (*mašaḥ*) this one" (16:12). This ritual marks the beginning of David's reign, but as with Saul, David is first anointed in private and only gradually receives the popular support that validates him as the king of Israel. He begins his kingship with a small power-base around Hebron, and after he expands from this base, he is anointed by the people as king over Judah (2 Sam 2:4). Finally, he is recognized as king over all of Israel and anointed by the people as such (2 Sam 5:1–4). This process shows that kingship in Israel was a function of both divine appointment and popular consent. David is the messiah as soon as he is anointed by Samuel, but he is not recognized as king by the people overnight. It took years for him to gain legitimacy among the people, and when they finally recognize him as their leader, it is the people themselves who anoint him as messiah.

The mirror image of this process is the decline of Saul, whose power diminishes as David's expands. Despite his rejection by God, Saul enjoyed some popular support until his death, and his son was even a legitimate rival of David for the throne. As such, Saul maintains his status as God's anointed, which even David recognizes. When Saul is killed in battle and his killer reports the news to David, he chastises the killer for "destroy[ing] the LORD's anointed" and even has him killed (2 Sam 1:14–16). David's reaction contains an important insight into the status of God's messiah. Namely, the anointing ritual is a sacramental act that remains efficacious even after the anointed one has lost the power to rule or been replaced by another messiah.

The climax of David's reign is the covenant that God makes with him in 2 Samuel 7. Having established his authority over all of Israel, founded Jerusalem as his capital, and brought the ark of the covenant into the city (2 Sam 5—6), David is now "settled in his house" (7:1), and the time is right for God to build on his success by ensuring similar success for his descendants. God guarantees this future by making a covenant with the house of David:

> the LORD declares to you that the LORD will make you a house. When your days are fulfilled and you lie down with your ancestors, I will raise up your offspring after you, who shall come forth from your body, and I will establish his kingdom. He shall build a house for my name, and I will establish the throne of his kingdom forever. I will be a father to him, and he shall be a son to me. When he commits iniquity, I will punish him with a rod such as mortals use, with blows inflicted by human beings. But I will not take my steadfast love from him, as I took it from Saul, whom I put away from before you. Your house and your kingdom shall be made sure forever before me; your throne shall be established forever. *(7:11b–16)*

God's promise to David plays on the multiple meanings of "house" (Heb. *bet*). It refers to both the king's physical house (i.e., the palace) but also to his dynastic house (i.e., his descendants, like "House of Tudor" in English). The word can also refer to God's house (i.e., the temple), which is mentioned a few verses before this passage (7:5). Thus, in this most important statement on kingship, God guarantees the security of David's throne for his own reign and for all posterity.

This covenant represents the resolution of the question of kingship in Israel. Israel will have a king, and the office will not diminish God's divine kingship because God has found in David a man after God's own heart and also because God is extending himself to David and his descendants in new ways. For example, God's declaration that "I will be a father to him, and he shall be a son to me" (7:14) is an extraordinary promise of intimate relationship. By adapting the covenantal formula "I will be their God and they shall be my people" to a royal context and transferring to the king the sonship that had defined the people of Israel (cf. Exod 4:22), God makes the king a partner in the divine plan and gives him the best possible chance for success.

Moreover, accepting that David and dynasty will not always live up to God's expectations, God makes allowances for their mistakes. God will punish their iniquity but will not take away from them the steadfast love (Heb. *ḥesed*) that was removed from Saul (7:15). As we saw in Chapter 2, Hebrew *ḥesed* denotes the loyalty between two covenantal partners; it is foundational for a committed relationship. The promise of unconditional *ḥesed*, which is offered in explicit contrast to God's relationship with Saul, suggests that God has learned that kingship will require divine mercy. The institution of kingship in Israel does not depend on the perfection of the kings themselves but upon the grace and mercy of God, who adopts the king as a son and accepts his imperfections—not with impunity but with forbearance to ensure the stability of the office.

This forbearance was put to the test almost immediately by David and later by his son Solomon. David had never been a man of spotless character; he was driven by self-interest, which sometimes led to poor or questionable decisions, like when he spent sixteen months fighting as a mercenary for the Philistines, who were Israel's archenemies at the time (1 Sam 27, 29). Of course, the narrator is careful to note that David never fought against his own people (27:8–11), just as the narrator always finds a way to distance David from the killing of his rivals (e.g., 2 Sam 3:26–28). Still, the shadow side of David's character is never quite dispelled. His shortcomings offer further confirmation of God's tendency in the Bible to choose leaders who are not perfect but, with God's help, become worthy of their vocation. Although David's ruddiness (1 Sam 16:12) and checkered history might suggest his unsuitability for kingship, God sees his potential differently (1 Sam 16:7, 12) and makes a covenant with him despite his shortcomings. According to this covenant, David and his descendants will be punished for their iniquity, but their throne will endure forever. Thus, when David commits adultery with Bathsheba and has her husband killed, he is punished by God but remains king (2 Sam 11—12).

Despite his flaws, David is remembered as a model king who walked in God's ways. He is literally the standard against which every other king is measured; as the history proceeds, the biblical writers introduce each new king of Judah with a formulaic notice about whether the king followed David's example (see 1 Kgs 11:4, 6; 15:3, 11; 2 Kgs 14:3; 16:2; etc.). That few kings meet his standard is a sign of his extraordinary talent as a leader, as is the failure of his successors to hold together the kingdom he consolidated. David's achievement looms large also in the royal psalms, which celebrate his unique status as God's son and the divine promises made to his dynasty (see Ps 89:19–37; see also Pss 18, 72, 132, 144).

Solomon, Jeroboam, and the Division of the Kingdom

David's successor, Solomon, strains God's covenantal promises to the breaking point. Although his reign begins as a model of wise leadership (1 Kgs 3:9, 12, 28; 4:29, 34; 10:4, 23), his kingship is ultimately marred by the very sins Moses (Deut 17) and Samuel (1 Sam 8) had warned about in their negative predictions about kings. Solomon conscripted forced labor, acquired hundreds of horses and chariots, amassed silver and gold, and married hundreds of foreign wives and concubines (1 Kgs 5:13; 10:21–22, 26; 11:1–3). This last example was especially problematic because he built shrines for his wives' native deities, thus undermining the exclusive devotion to the God of Israel, which lay at the heart of the covenant.

The combination of forced labor and indulgence of foreign gods leads to the division of the kingdom that David had unified. The split is announced by the prophet Ahijah when he meets Jeroboam, who had been Solomon's chief of forced labor but recently rebelled against the king (1 Kgs 11:26–28). In a symbolic action reminiscent of Saul tearing Samuel's robe, Ahijah tore his garment into twelve pieces and gave ten to Jeroboam along with this message from God: "I am about to tear the kingdom from the hand of Solomon, and will give you ten tribes. One will remain his for the sake of my servant David" (11:31–32; cf. 1 Sam 15:27–28). In accordance with the covenantal promises to David, God punishes Solomon by reducing his dominion but does not take away the kingdom altogether. Jeroboam's private appointment as king and the division of the kingdom are soon publicly affirmed, when Solomon's son Rehoboam refuses to ease his father's policy of forced labor but expands it (1 Kgs 12:1–11). The northern tribes respond by seceding from the house of David and declaring Jeroboam their king (12:12–20).

The secession of the northern tribes is a crucial turning point in the history of Israel. From this point till their destructions—the Northern Kingdom in 721 BCE and the Southern Kingdom in 586 BCE—Israel will exist as two separate kingdoms: Israel in the north and Judah in the south. Each kingdom will have its own king, its own capital, and as we shall see, its own temples. The long separation of Israel and Judah highlights David's extraordinary achievement in unifying them. The two regions differ in so many ways (geographically, religiously, economically, culturally) that it is astounding that David held them together as long as he did. The united monarchy, though short-lived, plays no small role in Israel's memory of David's preeminence; not only was he God's partner and adopted son, his reign was a symbol of unity that Israel never achieved again.

In the aftermath of the split between north and south, Jeroboam had a chance to serve as a legitimate king and was even made the partner in a royal covenant with God, but Jeroboam made a critical mistake at the outset of his reign. The covenant was conveyed through the same prophet, Ahijah, who had announced his kingship over the ten northern tribes. Speaking for God, he told Jeroboam, "I will be with you, and will build you an enduring house, as I built for David" (1 Kgs 11:38b). The crucial difference between the two covenants is that God's promises to Jeroboam were conditional. Unlike David, whose dynasty is assured forever, Jeroboam's enduring house depended on his obedience to God's commandments (11:38a). Jeroboam had a chance to be like David, but his failure to walk in God's ways led to a downfall even more ruinous than Saul's.

Jeroboam's decisive sin was his construction of two temples in his Northern Kingdom. Worried that if his people continued to worship in Jerusalem, they would rediscover their loyalty to the Davidic king, Jeroboam built temples at Dan and Bethel as alternatives to the Jerusalem temple. This sin seals the fate of Jeroboam, his dynasty, and the entire Northern Kingdom. Indeed, just as David serves as a positive benchmark for southern kings, Jeroboam serves as a negative one for northern kings. Almost every king after him is introduced with the formulaic notice that he continued the "sin of Jeroboam" (1 Kgs 15:34; 16:19, 26; 22:52; 2 Kgs 3:3; 10:29, 31; etc.), and Jeroboam's rival temples ultimately provide the explanation for why God allowed the Northern Kingdom to be destroyed by the Assyrian army in 721 BCE (2 Kgs 17:21–23).

In this way, kingship in the Bible never shook the ambivalence that defined its development in Israel. Except for David and two other southern kings (Hezekiah and Josiah) who try to root out illicit forms of worship, kings in both Israel and Judah failed to live up to God's expectations of their office. Their failure was not so different from the early false starts of Abimelech and Saul, who likewise fell short of the royal ideal that David later embodied. He had flaws, of course, but nonetheless exemplified the king's role as God's partner in the establishment of justice and righteousness throughout Israel. Despite these failures, however, the concept of Davidic kingship retained its luster, and the promises God made to David continued to inspire hope among God's people.

Looking Ahead: Kingship during the Exile and Beyond

Like so many biblical traditions, kingship undergoes a radical transformation after the destruction of Israel and Judah. Israel's end comes in 721 BCE when its capital falls and its people are deported to other parts of the Assyrian Empire. (This deportation is the basis of the so-called "ten lost tribes" of Israel— "ten" because that is the number that comprised the Northern

Kingdom, and "lost" because they are never heard from again.)
Its demise leaves Judah as the sole kingdom and, along with
Benjamin, the only tribe left of the original twelve. It will survive
until 586 BCE, when it is destroyed by the Babylonian army and
its people are deported to Babylon.

These two destructions mark the end of traditional kingship
but not its obliteration. A look at biblical books written during
the Babylonian Exile (586–539 BCE) shows various attempts
to adapt kingship to the new exilic reality. The first example
comes in the last four verses of the Book of Kings, where we
learn that King Jehoiachin, the next-to-last king of Judah, was
released from prison by the Babylonian king and given a seat of
honor among other exiled kings (2 Kgs 25:27–30). Interpreters
are divided on this scene: is Jehoiachin a glimmer of hope for
the Davidic line, which is diminished in exile but survives; or
does his dependence on the Babylonian king signify an accep-
tance of imperial control and the end of Davidic sovereignty?

I lean toward the more positive reading. After all, before
their destructions Israel and Judah had lived for centuries in the
shadow of Assyria and Babylon and had increasingly given their
autonomy (and tribute) to these empires. Jehoiachin's dependence is little different from his predecessors. More important
is the king's survival; despite all the destruction and loss, the
line of David endures for the future that God has in store for
his people. This Davidic hope is briefly realized in Jehoiachin's
grandson, Zerubbabel (Ezra 3:2; 1 Chr 3:17–19), who co-governs
the Jews who returned from exile to Jerusalem under Persian
rule. Although Zerubbabel is identified with royal duties and
symbols (Hag 2:21–23; Zech 4:6–10), he abruptly disappears
without a trace, leaving the high priest with whom he had
shared governing duties as the only Jewish authority figure. (The

high priest will remain so throughout the Persian period as well as the Hellenistic and Roman periods that follow.)

Other exilic writers adopt more radical approaches to Davidic kingship. In the Book of Isaiah, for example, God extends directly to the people the promises he made to David: "I will make with you (plural) an everlasting covenant, my steadfast, sure love (Heb. *ḥesed*) for David" (Isa 55:3). The prophet has not given up on the promise of God's everlasting *ḥesed* but reimagines it without the mediation of the Davidic king. Just as Jeremiah reconceived the Sinai covenant as written on the hearts of individual Israelites (31:33), the Isaian prophet makes the Davidic covenant directly available to the exiles who return to God.

Another exilic prophet who reimagines Israel without kingship is Ezekiel. Through him God expresses outrage at Israel's selfish and wicked "shepherds" (i.e., kings) and dismisses them; from now on God himself will care for the sheep (Ezek 34). In this way, Ezekiel returns Israel to the divine kingship that preceded the monarchy and which had been stressed by earlier prophets. In fact, Ezekiel carefully avoids even using the word "king," preferring instead the word "prince" (34:24; 37:25).

This history of kingship in the Old Testament provides indispensable background for understanding Jesus as the Davidic messiah. By the time we get to his lifetime during the Roman occupation, kingship had largely ceased to exist as a Jewish office of leadership. During the Hellenistic period that followed the Persian Empire, the Maccabean Revolt and Hasmonean Dynasty (167–63 BCE) marked a period of political autonomy, and some of the Hasmonean rulers took the title *basileus* (Greek for "king"). The title even continued into the Roman Empire beginning with Herod the Great (37–4 BCE), founder of the Herodian dynasty, but his authority as ruler was not a function of his office but his imperial patronage. Thus, even though the title "king" persisted in the centuries after the last Davidic heir, it no longer represented the political and religious authority it had once signified.

The concept of messiah, however, continued to inspire hope for Jews, who looked forward to a future Davidic king who would prevail over their enemies once and for all. The New Testament reveals Jesus as the fulfillment of this hope. Indeed, the title of messiah becomes attached to his very name; "Christ" is the Greek translation of Hebrew "messiah," so the name Jesus Christ identifies him as "the anointed one." As we have seen, the title denotes kingship, and it is one of several ways that the gospels identify Jesus as the heir to David's throne. In addition to Peter's confession of Jesus as the messiah (Mark 8:29; Matt 16:16; Luke 9:20), Matthew's genealogy (1:1–17) and the shouting crowds in Jerusalem who call Jesus king and "son of David" (Mark 11:10; Matt 21:9; Luke 19:38) identify him as the fulfillment of the promises God made to David. Related to Jesus' role as messiah is his proclamation of the kingdom (or reign) of God. That Jesus both identifies as king and emphasizes God's kingship resolves again the longstanding tension between divine and human kingship. Just as David was God's adopted son, Jesus is the son of God who fulfills the will of his father.

The Old Testament background of kingship also helps us appreciate the ways that Jesus reinterprets the traditional duties of Israel's king. Just as the exilic prophets reimagined kingship for their circumstances, Jesus redefines the role of messiah according to his particular mission. As we saw above, he lived in era when Jews were hoping for a messiah who would bring an end to their trials and deliver them from their enemies once and for all. The expectation that Jesus would fulfill this hope is expressed well by the men who meet the risen (but disguised) Jesus on the road to Emmaus: "But we had hoped he would be the one to redeem Israel" (Luke 24:21). Jesus responds: "Was it not necessary that the Messiah should suffer these things and then enter into his glory?" (24:26). Throughout the gospels Jesus teaches his disciples that his kingship differs from their messianic expectations. The kingdom he proclaims is defined by compassion, not power, and he is a messiah who will suffer in solidarity with outcasts before he at last triumphs in glory. It is a difficult teaching for the disciples to understand, but the redefinition itself is consistent with the larger biblical perspective on kingship. It was never a one-size-fits-all institution but arose in particular circumstances and was subsequently adapted to new contexts. Because God is always seeking relationship with God's people and because kingship is a way for God to interact with them, the office transformed as necessary for it to continue to play a role in the life and faith of God's people.

QUESTIONS *for* REFLECTION

To what extent does the Bible's ambivalence over kingship reflect our own struggle to balance divine and temporal authority?

David's kingship is the result of divine appointment and the people's recognition. How is this model of leadership operative in today's Church?

Hebrew *ḥesed* is a defining feature of both the Sinai and Davidic covenants. How is this word, which denotes divine and human fidelity to each other, relevant for Christians today?